Health Promotion in Hospital

A Practical Handbook for Nurses

Anita S McBride
BH (Hons), MA, RGN, MIHE
Associate Director,
Centre for Health Promotion Evaluation, Oxford

Scutari Press
London

A division of Scutari Projects Ltd., the publishing company of the Royal College of Nursing.

First published 1995

British Library Cataloguing in Publication Data
McBride, Anita S.
  Health Promotion in Hospital: Practical
  Handbook for Nurses
  I. Title
  613.07

  ISBN 1-873853-19-X

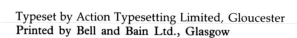

Typeset by Action Typesetting Limited, Gloucester
Printed by Bell and Bain Ltd., Glasgow

Contents

Preface

I believe nurses are ideally placed to promote preventative care and health promotion in hospital, in conjunction with the multidisciplinary team. After all, it is nurses who spend most of their time with patients.

(Senior staff nurse, general surgical ward)

Nurses . . . are not given the training, information or aids to do health promotion effectively . . . a lot is expected merely because we are nurses.

(Junior staff nurse, acute surgical ward)

Welcome to this practical handbook to guide you through the increasingly relevant area of health promotion. The overall aim of this handbook is to assist you, as a health-care professional working in a hospital, to establish a meaningful health promotion strategy in your area of practice. To achieve this, the handbook offers a wealth of resources: an understanding of the relevance of health promotion for hospital nurses, guidelines on how to implement health promotion in your area, knowledge and facts about lifestyle issues, and details of where further information relating to both lifestyle issues and effecting change may be found.

This handbook is unique in that it specifically addresses health promotion for patients in hospital. Obviously, a person is in hospital because of ill health, so general health promotion strategies may not always be appropriate and may even do the patient more harm than good. However, through empowering *you*, this handbook will help you to be better equipped to empower *patients* to make choices towards a healthier way of life.

Although written mainly for hospital nurses, this handbook will also prove a valuable resource for other health-care professionals.

Anita McBride

Acknowledgements

I am grateful to the Wolfson Centre for Prevention in Secondary Care, a three-year project funded by the Wolfson Foundation and particularly Dr Alex Gatherer, Project Director, for his continuing support and encouragement, and for initially conceiving the idea of a handbook.

I would also like to thank Louise Bean, Julie Holt, John McBride, Zelda Moorwood and the many nurses and hospital patients without whom the handbook would not exist.

This book is dedicated with gratitude for their support and encouragement to my parents, Roy and Diana Brown.

Acknowledgements

Introduction

Health promotion is becoming increasingly highlighted as an area in which much can be achieved to improve people's well-being. The *Health of the Nation* document from the Department of Health (1992) states that over the next decade, health gain will increasingly depend on prevention initiatives. There is a shift of emphasis, away from disease and illness as a focus, towards health. This applies not only in the community and primary care, where much has already been achieved (Fullard *et al*. 1984), but also in hospitals.

The World Health Organisation has introduced the concept of 'Health Promoting Hospitals', stressing health rather than disease. This involves two aspects: the roles of health-care professionals within the hospital and their relationship towards patients, and the hospital as an environment within which to work. The first strand channels how nurses work with patients to help them towards a healthier lifestyle, while the second influences hospital policies, such as 'no smoking' policies, and the choice of food available in the staff dining room.

WHAT IS HEALTH PROMOTION?

There are many conflicting definitions of health promotion in the literature, some more complicated than others (Tones *et al*. 1990). Although a new definition or a theoretical discussion will not be presented here, it is important to clarify how this term is used throughout the handbook.

Broadly speaking, there are two main approaches to health promotion: the 'traditional' and the 'modern'. The 'traditional' approach emphasises physical health and focuses on disease prevention, while the 'modern' approach stresses the promotion of positive health, which includes physical, mental and social aspects. This handbook is based upon the wider, more encompassing 'modern' approach.

Health promotion can also be defined as operating at two complementary levels – that of nurse – patient interaction and that of policy formulation – in both of which hospital nurses have a role to play. The chapters in this book covering lifestyle issues are specifically structured in such a way as to cover both these areas.

Health promotion is thus the process of enabling people to increase control over and improve their health in physical, mental and social terms. Although 'health' in its narrowest terms may be unachievable for hospital patients, there is no reason why people need not become *healthier*. In this way, health promotion becomes a positive activity, emphasising social, physical and mental resources, and removing the 'victim-blaming' and 'you must not . . .' stances. By taking a positive approach, nurses can promote good health and well-being as positive attributes, rather than focusing on the negative.

For example, at a recent 'no smoking day', a hospital nurse created a display in the main corridor of the hospital where she worked. As part of this, she put up a poster asking for ex-smokers to give tips on how they gave up smoking and what had helped them stay non-smokers. In this way she focused on the positive, asking for useful hints and constructive advice. She also found that the poster encouraged people who smoked to approach her, as they did not feel stigmatised as smokers in a non-smoking environment.

There is often confusion and dissension about 'health education' and 'health promotion' as concepts, both in the literature and among health-care professionals. Sometimes, the phrases are used interchangeably as meaning the same thing. However, in more precise terms, health education relates more to the direct giving of information and advice to patients. In contrast, health promotion reaches far wider, covering policy and environmental issues, both locally and nationally. For example, a local policy might relate to a 'no smoking' policy within a hospital, while a national policy might relate to the level of tax on a packet of cigarettes. Health promotion can also include issues of empowering patients and increasing their self-esteem, to help them to make informed decisions about their choice of lifestyle.

WHO SHOULD 'HEALTH PROMOTE'?

If, instead of 'health promotion', the concept becomes 'promoting health', what professional nurse could deny that he or she should be acting in this way? Promoting health is one of the basic concepts of nursing, both philosophically and in practice. The *Strategy for Nursing* from the Department of Health (1989) recommends that:

Health education and health promotion should be a recognised part of health care; *all* practitioners should develop skills in, and use *every* opportunity for, health promotion.

While much health promotion activity is disjointed (McBride 1992, Wilson-Barnett 1992), research has shown that hospital nurses feel professionally responsible and willing to take up this role. They are strongly supported by physiotherapists, dietitians and occupational therapists (McBride 1992), and these professions are keen to work together as a multidisciplinary team.

WHEN TO 'HEALTH PROMOTE'

If, as has been suggested, health promotion is seen as the process enabling people to increase control over, and improve, their health, the answer to the question 'When should health promotion take place?' can only be 'All the time'. The issue becomes not *what* is being said or done by the nurse but *how* it is said or done. Are patients being encouraged to be involved in their care to the best of their abilities, given their current state of health? Health promotion should become a way of nursing, an integral part of care.

HOW TO 'HEALTH PROMOTE'

Health promotion has already been discussed as a concept that needs to form part of all the nurse's activities with the patient. For this to be successful, health promotion needs to be seen as a complete strategy, not just a series of one-off activities. In this way, information and the approach taken will lessen the confusion and conflicting information given to patients.

For health promotion to succeed, it needs to be built around a model that includes evaluation, so that methods can be rigorously examined for their effectiveness. Too often, reliance is placed on an inherent feeling that something must work well because it is a 'good idea' and that results are being achieved without precisely defining the objectives of the intervention or objectively evaluating the outcome.

How to plan, implement and evaluate health promotion will be discussed further in Chapter 2.

HEALTH PROMOTION IN HOSPITAL

It has been suggested that hospital admission is a stressful time for patients, so health promotion is inappropriate. However, admission to hospital often acts as a catalyst for change, increasing motivation, a situation that is not replicated in primary care. Following a myocardial infarction, the patient and family often ask 'Why?' and 'What should we have done to prevent this?' This can be used to advantage by identifying those open to change and beginning a health promotion programme, which should be presented in a positive, non-blaming manner.

However, hospital patients do not have the same on-going continuity of care that happens in primary care. This needs to be addressed as part of the overall health promotion strategy, for example by implementing a referral system whereby patients with coronary heart disease are referred by ward nurses to practice nurses as part of the routine discharge procedure. This would involve links with primary care and provide follow-up and continuity, while capitalising on the advantages of routine practices in hospital care in the identification of 'at risk' patients.

HEALTH PROMOTION POLICIES

So far, this chapter has concentrated predominantly on nurse – patient interactions, but health promotion stretches far wider than this, to include policies that promote health. Unless these are seen as part of a health promotion strategy, patients can receive conflicting messages. For example, patients may be encouraged to reduce their smoking or refused surgery unless they stop smoking, yet the ward dayroom may permit smoking. A smoking policy that, for example, restricts smoking to very specific areas helps patients to achieve their targets. In this way, the 'healthy option' can start to become the 'easy option' rather than the 'hard option'. Policy issues are discussed further in Part Two in relation to particular lifestyle issues.

ABOUT THIS HANDBOOK

This book is set out as a handbook, which means that it is not designed to be read from cover to cover in the order that it is presented – although there is nothing to stop the book being read in this manner.

The handbook is designed so that it can be referred to as a resource when specific issues related to health promotion present themselves. The book is, therefore, divided into three different sections.

Part One covers the importance and relevance of health promotion in relation to nursing practice in hospital. Next, it examines how to formulate and then implement strategies. Real examples are used to illustrate how this can be achieved in practice. Difficulties highlighted by hospital nurses are presented, along with possible solutions that other nurses have developed. Thus, this section is practice based, founded on real situations and not academic theories.

Part Two examines the particular lifestyle issues of smoking, alcohol, nutrition and physical activity in depth, covering their effects on patients physically, psychologically and socially, together with specific diseases that are related to them. From this, strategies are suggested to help patients towards a healthier choice, whether this is in physical, psychological or social terms. Policy issues are also presented, in relation to both patients within the hospital and staff for whom the hospital is a work environment.

The third section, the Appendices, assists follow-up of issues highlighted by the rest of the handbook. It supplies contact addresses where further information about a particular topic may be found and also organisations that nurses might find useful to develop their health promotion skills further, either through informal or academic courses. A reading list is also provided.

REFERENCES

Department of Health (1989) *A Strategy for Nursing: A Report of the Steering Committee.* London: Department of Health, Nursing Division.
Department of Health (1992) *Health of the Nation: A Strategy for England.* London: HMSO.
Fullard E, Fowler G & Gray J (1984) Facilitating prevention in primary care. *British Medical Journal* **298:** 1582–7.
McBride A (1992) *Developing an Effective Nursing Health Promotion Strategy for Adult Patients on Acute Wards.* Paper presented to 'Promoting Health: International Research Conference for Nursing', London, September 1992.
Tones K, Tilford S & Robinson Y (1990) *Health Education: Effectiveness and Efficiency.* London: Chapman and Hall.
Wilson-Barnett J (1992) *Factors Influencing Health Education and Health Promotion Practice in Acute Ward Areas.* Paper presented to 'Promoting Health: International Research Conference for Nursing', London, September 1992.

Part One

The Hospital Nurse and Health Promotion

1

The Scope of Health Promotion

Health promotion is not just about helping individual people to change their lifestyles. Although this is important, the way in which we live is more than our individual actions, it is about the type of world we live in and the policies that create this world. Health promotion can, therefore, be summarised as health education plus healthy public policy. Healthy public policies are those policies which work towards people being healthier, and can range from restricting chemical use to increasing tax on cigarettes. This is not necessarily an easy task, as there is sometimes a conflict of interests. For example, nuclear power reactors may be considered as a resource to encourage as they save natural resources, but may also be seen as a resource to discourage owing to the possible harm caused to people working and living nearby. In this way, health promotion is not just the responsibility of health-care professionals but involves everyone through their work and their choices in political elections.

'Health for All by the Year 2000' is a strategy developed by the World Health Organisation (WHO) to improve health. The aim is to concentrate on avoiding disease through:

- the promotion of healthy lifestyles;
- a reduction in preventable diseases;
- the provision of comprehensive health coverage for the whole population.

THE OTTAWA CHARTER: AN INTERNATIONAL STRATEGY

The Ottawa Charter (World Health Organisation 1986) is a charter for action to achieve health that grew out of 'Health for All by the Year 2000'. In a series of statements, the Charter defines health promotion action as:

3

- building healthy public policy through legislation, tax, income and social policies, and organisational change;
- creating supportive environments by conserving natural resources throughout the world;
- empowering communities to give them ownership and control over their health and well-being;
- enabling people to develop personal skills and helping them to make healthy choices, based on knowledge and understanding;
- reorienting health services towards health promotion rather than only taking responsibility for clinical and curative services.

HEALTH OF THE NATION: A NATIONAL STRATEGY

Health of the Nation is a strategy document for England, produced in 1992 by the Government; similar strategies exist for Scotland, Wales and Northern Ireland. This document sets out, for the first time ever in England, targets for improving the nation's health. The Department of Health states that promoting good health and preventing ill health are equally as important as treating illness.

Health of the Nation has its roots in a number of national and international initiatives aimed at improving health, including 'Health for All by the Year 2000'.

The strategy aims to achieve success by:

- concentrating on major health problems;
- focusing on promoting good health and preventing disease as much as on care and treatment;
- accepting the need to work in partnership with individuals, communities, health professionals and policy makers.

The strategy focuses on five main key areas:

- Coronary heart disease and strokes.
- Cancer.
- Mental illness.
- Accidents.
- HIV/AIDS and sexual health.

These key areas were chosen as they are all major causes of serious illness or early death and offer scope for effective action. A series of targets has been set within each key area, to give a sense of direction to the efforts to improve health and to focus attention on areas where it is felt progress can be made. The targets are a set of statements of what is to be achieved by a specific date.

The effects of any health promotion strategy are difficult to measure and evaluate in the short term, so the rate of progress towards achieving these targets needs to be measured in years rather than months.

According to *Health of the Nation: One Year On* ... (Department of Health 1993a), the first year of the strategy has been positive. There has been movement towards achieving the targets in most of the key areas, and the momentum appears to be building, as more agencies and individuals become involved.

TARGETING CORONARY HEART DISEASE AND STROKES

Coronary heart disease is the single largest cause of death, being responsible for 26% of all deaths in England in 1991. Strokes caused 12% of all deaths in England in the same year and are also a major cause of disability. Although the rate of coronary heart disease in England has been declining since the 1970s, it is still one of the highest in the world, yet much heart disease is preventable. The main risk factors for coronary heart disease and stroke are cigarette smoking, raised blood cholesterol and lack of exercise, all of which can be influenced by changes in behaviour. Government targets, to be achieved by the year 2000, include:

- reducing the mortality from coronary heart disease and stroke of people under 65 by at least 40%;
- reducing the mortality from coronary heart disease for people between the ages of 65 and 74 by at least 30%;
- reducing the mortality from stroke for people between the ages of 65 and 74 by 40%.

These targets take 1990 as the year for baseline data. They all focus on death rather than illness, because it is easier to measure and, therefore, less controversial.

TARGETING CANCER

Cancer was responsible for 25% of all deaths in England in 1991. Smoking is a major risk factor, contributing to 30% of all deaths from cancer and 80% of deaths from lung cancer. There is also increasing evidence that diet is associated with some types of cancer, for example cancer of the stomach, large bowel and reproductive system. Obesity appears to be associated with cancer of the gall bladder and uterus.

Government targets concerning cancer include:

- reducing the mortality from lung cancer in people under the age of 75 by at least 30% for men and 15% for women by the year 2010;

- reducing the incidence of invasive cancer of the cervix by at least 20% by the year 2000.

Targets focusing on diseases are translated into targets for specific lifestyle issues as a recognition of the importance of lifestyle in affecting morbidity and mortality.

TARGETING LIFESTYLE

Targets set for changes in lifestyle aimed at preventing disease and death include the following:

Smoking

Using baseline data from 1990, targets to be achieved by the year 2000 include:

- reducing the number of people who smoke by 20%;
- reducing the consumption of cigarettes by at least 40%;
- at least 33% of women smokers to stop smoking at the start of their pregnancy.

Nutrition

Using a baseline year of 1990, targets to be achieved by the year 2005 include:

- reducing the average saturated fat intake by at least 35%;
- reducing the average fat intake by at least 12%;
- reducing the proportion of adults who are obese by 25% for men and 33% for women. This would mean no more than 6% of men and 8% of women being obese.

Alcohol

Again, using baseline data from 1990, targets to be achieved by the year 2005 include:

- reducing the proportion of men who drink more than 21 units per week by 30%, which would mean no more than 18% of men drinking more than this.
- reducing the proportion of women who drink more than 14 units per week by 30%, meaning that no more than 8% of women would drink more than this.

Physical activity

Physical activity contributes to health; lack of exercise contributes to ill health. However, targets have not yet been set for physical activity, as there is considered to be insufficient information available about current levels of fitness in the population.

HEALTHY ALLIANCES

The main thrust of health promotion in the past has been from within community settings, where health promotion units have worked alongside health professionals. However, with the advent of the 'Health of the Nation' strategy, there has been a need for all agencies to form closer links and work together. This has come to be known as 'Healthy Alliances', based on the concept that social, environmental and institutional changes are essential in promoting the health of individual people. The purpose of healthy alliances is to involve as much of the population as possible in achieving the targets set in the five key areas by focusing on a variety of settings such as:

- healthy cities;
- healthy schools;
- healthy hospitals;
- healthy workplaces;
- healthy prisons;
- healthy environments.

There are two strands within this settings approach:

- Similar types of setting, for example two hospitals, form networks with each other.
- Different types of settings, for example a hospital and a school, form alliances with each other.

Hospital staff have a unique opportunity to develop health promotion strategies that benefit not only patients and clients but also staff themselves. The WHO has developed a Health Promoting Hospital initiative that has spread throughout the European Community, with a 'model' hospital in each country.

HEALTH PROMOTING HOSPITALS

The Health Promoting Hospital initiative aims to promote positive health and well-being, both in the hospital itself and outwards to the community that it serves. As well as the formal 'model' concept of the WHO, many other initiatives are being developed to provide health promotion within hospital settings.

THE ROLE OF THE HOSPITAL NURSE IN HEALTH PROMOTION

Both the Department of Health (1989) and the Royal College of Nursing (1989) have highlighted the necessity for nurses to develop skills in the areas of health education and health promotion. However, research into health promotion in acute care settings has shown that little has been achieved (Wilson-Barnett and Latter 1993), suggesting that nurses in acute settings are often not fulfilling their potential in the area of health promotion (McBride 1994).

Both the latter studies highlighted the fact that nurses were interested and committed to the concept of health promotion but were limited by resources and knowledge of how to promote health. Therefore, before nurses begin to enable patients to change their lifestyle, they need to enable the profession to become health promoting. In *Targeting Practice: The Contribution of Nurses, Midwives and Health Visitors* (Department of Health 1993b), the implications for nursing and midwifery education are highlighted, stating that in order to provide quality health promotion, the key concepts of health promotion need to be fundamental in both pre-registration education and post-registration courses.

THE FOCUS OF HEALTH PROMOTION IN HOSPITAL

Health promotion strategies are sometimes categorised into three different levels:

- *Primary prevention* – the removal of the cause of a disease. For example, a smoking cessation group helps people to stop smoking, thus removing cigarettes, implicated in the cause of many diseases.
- *Secondary prevention* – the early detection of disease before symptoms are apparent, for example the detection of hypertension, which is a risk factor for coronary heart disease.
- *Tertiary prevention* – the management of disease, with the emphasis on preventing deterioration in the patient's condition, for example the management of a patient with diabetes to limit the effects of the illness.

The initial reaction of hospital nurses can be one of thinking that their role is mainly in the area of tertiary prevention, ie disease management. Indeed, much of a hospital nurse's work is in this area, yet there is plenty of scope before a patient's condition has reached this stage. Many patients in hospital may have risk factors associated with their lifestyle that are not directly connected with the reason for their admission. For example, a patient may be found to be a heavy smoker when admitted with appendicitis. Although not directly related to this particular admission, smoking will affect the risks of anaesthetic, the recovery and the patient's future risks of disease.

Health promotion can focus on disease or on lifestyle issues. A disease focus could be coronary heart disease, the risk factors then including smoking, lack of exercise and diet. A risk factor focus could be nutrition, which can then be linked to coronary heart disease, cancer and dental disease. The disease focus is negative in outlook and neglects the patient as a complete being. However, care must be taken with a risk focus not to neglect the patient's medical condition and prognosis when planning health promotion interventions.

ETHICAL ISSUES

Often, people do not feel happy about coming into hospital but they should not be made to feel worse by hospital staff not valuing them because of the way they live.

Underlying health promotion is the concept that the health-care professional knows what is best for the patient in terms of health behaviour, yet knowledge and 'facts' change over time. For example, nutrition education campaigns in the 1950s encouraged people to eat eggs and red meat, while current understanding encourages limiting eating these products.

Health promotion at the right time is appropriate. For example, one particular hospital is planning to ask patients coming into hospital for elective surgery whether they would like help to stop smoking, ie hospitals are being selective in whom they approach, and patients are being offered a choice. Information at the wrong time is inappropriate. For example, a recent poster has the slogan 'Don't drink and drive', together with a picture of a smashed peach. This was found in a waiting room beside the hospital chapel where recently bereaved relatives sat.

There is also the temptation to exaggerate the effects of a particular activity in improving health or preventing ill-health in order to encourage patients to change their behaviour.

In summary:

- Can you justify why a particular patient's lifestyle should change?
- Do you know the facts? Are they research based?
- Is a change in lifestyle appropriate for a particular patient in the context of his or her life and prognosis?
- Are you being honest with the patient?

- Are you being realistic?
- Is the patient making an informed choice or being bullied? Although both approaches may change attitudes and behaviour, are they both ethical?

Although these points have been described in relation to patients, the same ethical principles apply to staff and visitors, too.

THE NURSE AS A ROLE MODEL

Should nurses who smoke or know they drink too much alcohol attempt to influence patients' lifestyles? Although the ideal would be for all nurses to be role models, few would be able to fulfil this position. However, instead of shying away from these issues, nurses can:

- admit they are not ideal; honesty can increase respect;
- turn their problem to advantage; for example, patients may feel that a nurse who is overweight and struggling to lose weight is more empathetic than a slim nurse;
- use the opportunity to reconsider their own lifestyle.

REFERENCES

Department of Health (1989) *A Strategy for Nursing: A Report of the Steering Committee*. London: Department of Health Nursing Division.

Department of Health (1992) *Health of the Nation: A Strategy for England*. London: HMSO.

Department of Health (1993a) *One Year On . . .* London: HMSO.

Department of Health (1993b) *Targeting Practice: The Contribution of Nurses, Midwives and Health Visitors*. London: Department of Health.

McBride A (1994) Health promotion in hospitals: The attitudes, beliefs and practices of hospital nurses. *Journal of Advanced Nursing*, **20**: 92–100.

Royal College of Nursing (1989) *Into the Nineties: Promoting Professional Excellence*. London: Royal College of Nursing.

Wilson-Barnett J & Latter S (1993) Factors influencing nurses' health education and health promotion practice in acute ward areas. In Wilson-Barnett J & Macleod-Clark J (eds), *Research in Health Promotion and Nursing*. London: Macmillan.

World Health Organisation (1986) *Ottawa Charter for Health Promotion*. Geneva: World Health Organisation.

2

Strategies for Health Promotion

Strategies for health promotion depend on the view of what health promotion is about. A variety of theoretical health promotion models have been developed to explain health and health promotion. However, for practical health promotion, there are three main areas that can be focused on, whether for staff, patients or visitors:

- Changing attitudes.
- Changing behaviour.
- Changing the environment.

CHANGING ATTITUDES

A change in attitude does not necessarily mean that a change in behaviour follows as a direct consequence. Theories and research conclusions vary as to what an attitude is and, therefore, how it may be changed. However, for practical purposes, attitudes can be described as views affected by beliefs and values, which may be reflected in behaviour. Thus, attitudes can be changed by a challenge to a person's knowledge or value base, or by altering their behaviour. Health promotion initiatives have used both of these approaches.

Although attitudes are relatively stable, they are not fixed, so there is the potential for change. If an attitude is approved of by others, it is reinforced, so becomes stronger. Thus, attitudes can be changed by:

- presenting the patient with new information that is inconsistent with their current beliefs;
- making the patient behave in a manner that is inconsistent with their current beliefs.

Although both these approaches challenge current beliefs, the first empowers patients by giving them information and, therefore, the opportunity to make informed choices about their behaviour; this could be, for example, by explaining the effects of cigarette smoke on the lungs. The second approach dominates patients by forcing them to behave in a certain manner, for example by banning smoking on hospital premises.

CHANGING BEHAVIOUR

Before someone is prepared to change their behaviour to reduce their risk of disease, that person needs to accept that behaviour affects the risk of disease and that diseases are not solely the result of immutable factors such as fate, chance, genes or God. Fatalism may stem from religion: Moslems tend to display a fatalistic view of the future, which is believed to be largely under the control of the Will of Allah.

There can be difficulties over changing behaviour for some lifestyle issues. Most people would accept the links between smoking and disease, but not, for example, some aspects of nutritional advice. Experts themselves disagree on the implications of nutrition, and opinions have changed over time, leading people to suspect that current theories will change too. The only acceptable stance for the nurse is to be honest with the patient, otherwise credibility is lost and the ethics of the situation become doubtful. This honesty can be achieved by using such words as 'probable', 'likely' or 'possible'.

As well as understanding the connections between behaviour and disease, patients need to accept that their behaviour increases their risk of disease. Patients are more likely to change their behaviour if the nurse:

- demonstrates the short term benefits, for example explaining to patients that their health will improve as soon as they start losing weight;
- emphasises the positive benefits as well as the reduction in the risk of illness. For example, by giving up smoking, the patient will feel better, smell nicer and have more money to spend on other things;
- practises good communication skills;
- helps the patient to reduce the psychological costs of behaviour change through exploring alternatives. For example, a patient may be reluctant to drink less alcohol because it helps relaxation, but a new hobby could be relaxing if appropriate and appealing to the patient.

CHANGING THE ENVIRONMENT

Changing the environment can offer two areas of health benefit for patients, visitors and staff:

- The environment itself can become healthier. For example, a no-smoking environment prevents the risks of passive smoking while in the hospital.
- Healthier behaviour can be made easier. For example, if sports equipment and areas are provided on the hospital site, staff are more likely to exercise than if they have to travel to a more distant sports centre.

It may not be easy to change the environment, particularly if costs are involved, but it can be done. It is more likely that the environment will be changed if:

- benefits to health can be demonstrated;
- a written policy involving all disciplines is developed;
- costs can be offset, for example by charging to use sports equipment;
- there is support from professional bodies or if they are also campaigning for a specific change. Nurses are professional experts in their field and can use this to influence others. A multidisciplinary approach can be even more effective, as use of professional networks can widen the sphere of influence;
- there is a government-led initiative highlighting a specific issue. This increases awareness among people and can offer publicity on a wide scale.

SETTING PRIORITIES

Health promotion can aim to:

- change a patient's behaviour towards a healthier lifestyle, as defined by health-care professionals;
- change a patient's attitude through education and informed choice towards a healthier lifestyle, as defined by health-care professionals;
- change the hospital towards being a healthier environment;
- identify patients' concerns and address what, if anything, they want to do about it;
- prevent or ameliorate disease through early detection and treatment.

Rather than trying to 'change the world', it is more realistic to decide on priorities for health promotion and use these to form the basis of a strategy. To do this, it is helpful to answer these questions:

- What is your aim? (This is discussed in the next section.)
- Whom do you want to aim health promotion towards: patients, visitors, ward/department staff, the whole hospital?
- Do you want to aim at all the people in the above group or do you wish to define it more narrowly:

  - by age;
  - by disease;
  - by risk, for example, smokers, patients with hypertension or those with a low income?

- If patients are the focus, are you trying to reduce the effects of established disease pathology or are you aiming to prevent disease?
- Why have you chosen your particular aims? Establish the reasons for your choice; this helps you to clarify what you are trying to achieve.

Having decided your priorities:

- Is this strategy feasible? Are the necessary skills and resources available?
- Is there research in this area to highlight successes and failures for health promotion?
- Are others already addressing this need? Will this conflict with their work? Can you work together as a joint initiative, for example by working with dietitians and catering staff to develop a nutritional policy.

AIMS AND OBJECTIVES

Once you have determined your priorities, you can then go on to set aims and objectives. These are not an academic exercise but are crucial to give you a focus on what you are setting out to achieve in health promotion. The aims (or aim) are broad statements of what you are trying to achieve – they are the goals. Objectives are much more specific and are the results or outcomes to be achieved within a specific time (*see* Figure 4, p.26).

Having established your aims and objectives, the next stage is to turn these into action. There are a variety of methods that you could use:

- giving a talk to a group of patients, visitors or staff;
- running a workshop where those attending participate;
- one-to-one discussion;
- setting up a display or exhibition in the hospital;
- using a leaflet or producing your own.

The decision on the type of method to use depends on:

- your aims and objectives. Sometimes these do not leave much scope for different methods, and some methods are usually more appropriate than others;
- acceptability to those you are trying to influence. For example, patients may be reluctant to discuss personal issues in a group setting;
- the amount of time you have available. For example, one-to-one discussion is time-consuming if you wish to involve many patients;
- cost;
- access to resources.

RESOURCES

There are a variety of resources that you can use to assist you. These include:

- other people who can help you directly:

    - nurses;
    - experts in different disciplines, for example, dietitians and physiotherapists;
    - patients: they have experiences that you can draw on;
    - technical staff, for example computer operators and artists;
    - a health promotion facilitator;
    - health promotion unit staff;

- existing policies and plans, which can be useful to set the scene of your work and as a back-up;
- other people who have an effect on those you are trying to influence, for example, other patients, relatives, friends and self-help groups;
- existing facilities and services. Find out what already exists, as these can reinforce your work and help you to ensure that you do not waste your expertise duplicating an existing programme.

EVALUATION

Evaluation is essential in order to ascertain the effectiveness of an intervention in achieving its aims. It may seem strange to consider evaluation before you have actually done anything, but planning the evaluation at this stage is much easier and more beneficial than leaving it until the health promotion intervention has begun.

The reasons for evaluating health promotion activities are:

- To ensure that the programme is having the desired effect. Without evaluation, it is not known whether the activity is having the right effect or, indeed, any effect at all. This knowledge can be used as an indicator of how to improve areas that are less successful and reinforces the worthiness of successful activities.
- To assess cost-effectiveness, both in terms of time and money. Resources can be channelled into activities with most benefit.
- To improve methods and materials. Different materials, approaches and ideas can be assessed and compared for effectiveness.
- To assess the validity of health promotion as a nursing intervention.
- To assess whether or not activities are ethically appropriate. Is it justifiable to expect hospital patients to consider changing their lifestyle?

As well as considering why evaluation should be carried out, other factors to be taken into account are as follows:

- When to carry out the evaluation. The activity could be evaluated while the patient is still in hospital or at a later date after discharge, depending on whether short- or long-term outcomes and effects are seen as the focus of the activity.
- What to evaluate. It is difficult to separate out the effect of a particular activity from the rest of nursing care, so it is important to be aware of what to evaluate and that this is feasible. For example, a nurse could evaluate the reactions of patients to a leaflet encouraging them to stop smoking and assess its effectiveness. It would, however, be impossible to prove that a particular leaflet made someone stop smoking, as a change in behaviour can be from a variety of causes.
- Is it to be an evaluation of the *process* (for example, were the appropriate methods and materials used during a teaching session?) or the *outcome* of the intervention (for example, did the nurses in the teaching session increase their knowledge of lifestyle issues)?
- How to evaluate. This can be done by a variety of methods, depending on what is to be evaluated, for example:

- an audit of nursing notes for mention of health promotion interventions;
- a questionnaire for patients asking about health promotion interventions, either in general or specifically;
- a simple count of leaflets taken from a display;
- observing and recording behaviour to assess changes;
- examining new policy documents and comparing them with previous documentation;
- interviews with staff and patients to ascertain their knowledge, attitudes, beliefs and practices.

- Who the evaluation is for. If it is to assess how effective the intervention was and how it could be improved for next time, a few notes may be adequate. If, however, the report is for someone else, for example the nursing manager or a funding body, more detail will be needed, and the types of question that they will raise will need to be considered.
- Is it beneficial to carry out an evaluation prior to the intervention? Change cannot be measured adequately without an initial assessment, which provides a baseline for comparisons.

An example of a simple evaluation tool, a questionnaire for patients to consider the effectiveness of health promotion leaflets, is given in Figure 1.

Experiment with the wording of questions to see which gives the most helpful information. For example, people do not generally like to be negative, so asking what they did *not* like is unlikely to give much information. Instead, asking what they would like to change is likely to be far more helpful. This way, readers may also offer solutions rather than just highlighting problems to be addressed.

It should be remembered that patients and others do not have to complete any questionnaires or answer questions. Their voluntary cooperation and willingness need to be gained. In practice, this is often best achieved by explaining why the questions are being asked and what is going to happen to the information. People are often both happier and more honest if they are guaranteed anonymity, so no-one knows which answers they have given.

If patients are to be questioned ethical committee approval may need to be ensured. This can be checked with the local ethical committee, who can also give information of how to go about eliciting approval.

Please tick as appropriate

Have you been given leaflets or other written information on smoking?

YES/NO

If yes: Have you read it/them?

    [   ]   Yes, all
    [   ]   Yes, mostly
    [   ]   Just flicked through
    [   ]   No, not read

How useful did you find it/them?

    [   ]   Very useful
    [   ]   Quite useful
    [   ]   Not really useful

Please make any comments about the leaflet(s) that you think may be

helpful to us ....

....

....

....

....

THANK YOU

Fig. 1   Patient questionnaire on the effectiveness of health promotion leaflets

TAKING ACTION

Having decided on your:

- aims and objectives and the most appropriate way to achieve them;
- and how to evaluate your intervention;

you can now formulate a detailed plan of action. This should cover:

- what is going to be done;
- who is going to do what;
- what resources are going to be required;

- when the intervention is going to happen;
- where this will ocurr.

This then becomes the guide towards fulfilling your aims, and you are ready to act. An example of a health promotion strategy in this format is given later in this chapter.

COMMUNICATION SKILLS

To improve the chance of patients' changing their behaviour:

- check the patient's existing understanding and attitudes towards the issue;
- give information and advice early in the discussion, as it is more likely to be remembered then;
- use short words and sentences;
- arrange the information into categories;
- do not expect too much. For example, it is difficult to help a patient to give up smoking if he is anxious about his marriage;
- tackle one issue at a time;
- repeat the information and advice several times;
- give specific concrete information and advice rather than general instructions or suggestions;
- check that the patient has understood;
- encourage other health-care professionals to reinforce what has been said;
- record what has been said in the patient's notes to act as a reminder to you and to inform other ward staff. This helps to ensure consistency for the patient.

When a patient is not fluent in English, other strategies are needed to achieve effective communication:

- Speak clearly and slowly.
- Allow time for the patient to try to grasp what is being said.
- Use simple words and repeat them. Avoid using a variety of words to mean the same thing, as this can add to the confusion.
- Avoid slang and idiom; these are culturally understood, so literal translations are often complete nonsense.
- Pictures and mime can be helpful.
- Check that the patient understands. Do not use closed questions that require yes/no answers, as these can be misleading.
- There may be someone working in the hospital who can speak the language. Many hospitals have developed a list of language skills among their staff.

- Try learning another language. This can be particularly worthwhile if you nurse many people who speak the same language; some local authorities run relevant courses.
- Talk to the patient's visitors, as they may speak English and be able to translate.

WORKSHOPS AND TALKS

Workshops and talks can be for staff, patients, relatives or a combination of these. They can be used to:

- give information, by, for example, a physiotherapy talk to nurses advising on exercises to strengthen back muscles;
- provide a forum for discussion, for example a health promotion interest group for hospital staff;
- develop skills, by, for example, a workshop on how to produce effective posters;
- give mutual support, for example for patients or staff trying to give up smoking.

In setting up a group, aims and objectives need to be identified so that an appropriate strategy can be planned. The aims and objectives of group members may be different from those of the leader, who will be more effective by being aware of the different needs of participants. These needs can be taken into account when planning how to run the group, or some people may be excluded as being inappropriate for the group.
Other issues to consider are:

- leadership style. Do you want to be directive or act as a facilitator, where the group is more participative? The most appropriate style depends on the leader's personality, the previous experiences of group members and the aims of the group;
- where the group will meet. Are the facilities appropriate? Are disturbances likely? For example, it can be very difficult to run a session in the ward office as the telephone is likely to be a distraction;
- the layout of the room. Groups work best when people can sit in a circle, so that everyone is physically included in the group and can see everyone else.

EXAMPLE OF A WORKSHOP PLAN

A hospital nurse with an interest in health promotion was asked to run a workshop for hospital nurses as part of a post-basic course on using patient education literature. First, he clarified the topic, who his audience were and how long his session was allotted:

- *Title*: Utilising Health Promotion Education Literature: Strategies for Incorporating into Care.
- *Group*: 10 nurses on the Critical Care Course.
- *Duration*: 1 hour.

He then formulated his aim:

- To enable nurses to make effective use of written material to enhance their health promotion role.

and from this, his objectives for the session:

- Nurses will be able to:

1) List the advantages and disadvantages of using written or printed patient education literature.
2) State how this could be used in their area of work.

Having determined these, the nurse planned the session in detail, as shown in Figure 2.

---

1. Introduction
Welcome and discussion of session aims and objectives.

2. a. Why educate patients?
Group discussion based on personal experiences and relevant literature.

b. Advantages and disadvantages of using literature
i. Identify personal experiences of receiving information and discuss good and bad points.
ii. Group exercise. 3 groups receive a set of directions.
   Group 1 – listening only.
   Group 2 – listening and taking notes.
   Group 3 – listening and being given leaflet.
   Check and compare recall.
   Draw conclusions – use references on overhead projection and handout.
iii. Brainstorm advantages and disadvantages of using literature, based on group exercise.

c. Consideration of in-house literature
i. Discuss how literature is compiled and give examples. Use handout.
ii. Get group to relate the above to their own areas of practice.

3. Conclusion
Summarise the main points.
Answer group questions.

Fig. 2 Example of a workshop plan

LEAFLETS

Using leaflets is a popular way of getting health promotion information across to patients. The advantage of leaflets is that they can act as a reminder and reinforce information and advice at a later time. However, to be successful they must:

- be relevant to the patient's particular personal needs;
- give appropriate information and advice, of the appropriate depth for the reader;
- use language that is most apt for the reader.

There are, however, disadvantages in using leaflets, although these can be overcome with care:

- They may not be appropriate.
- The nurse cannot check the patient's understanding.
- Leaflets are unhelpful for those who cannot read or who are unlikely to be motivated enough to apply themselves to understanding the content.
- Simply giving a patient a leaflet does not allow for discussion, so the context of using leaflets needs to be considered.

Developing your own leaflets for patients

Ideally, a leaflet will summarise guidance given orally by the nurse to each patient, individually tailored to that patient's particular needs, but this is obviously impossible. Thus, leaflets need to be designed to be appropriate to a specific group of patients. This could be organised by lifestyle issues and/or conditions. The choice depends on:

- the type of area/ward worked in;
- the types of commonly presented condition;
- the lifestyle issues that frequently arise among the patients.

However, there are general guidelines that apply to leaflets for patients. They should cover:

- the seriousness of the problem, without causing excess anxiety. For example, it is acceptable to say that smoking causes lung cancer but not appropriate to describe the experience of the terminal stages of such a cancer;
- the risks to the particular patient reading the leaflet;
- the benefits of changing lifestyle behaviour;

- the difficulties of changing lifestyle behaviour and how these may be overcome.

Other issues to consider are:

- the language used, which should not be too technical or medical but also should not patronise;
- the use of short sentences that are clear and straightforward;
- legibility of the print: is it easy to read?
- avoiding general advice. Be specific and precise;
- evaluating the leaflet. Try it out and take note of positive criticism and suggestions;
- its effectiveness – if it is effective, share it with others.

POSTERS AND DISPLAYS

Posters and displays can be a useful method of promoting health to a wide audience. They can:

- raise awareness of health promotion issues;
- challenge attitudes and behaviour;
- give information and highlight other resources for more information, for example addresses of organisations;
- invite people to pick up a leaflet;
- be reused at various sites or at different times.

There are disadvantages to using posters and displays, although these can often be overcome:

- Anyone passing may read the poster, so the content needs to reflect the likely audience, which will depend on the site selected. A ward-based poster may attract staff, patients and visitors, while a poster in a nurses' home will have nurses as its main readership.
- Commercially-produced posters can be expensive to buy and may contain advertising.
- Posters and displays can deteriorate and get damaged, particularly in areas where there are many people passing.
- High quality materials can be expensive.

Developing your own posters and displays

Unlike leaflets, posters and displays cannot be tailored to particular groups. The only control over who reads them is by the siting of the poster or display. This, in turn, will have an effect on the content of the material. Is the health promotion aimed at all who pass or at a particular group of people? The choice of site may be a limiting factor (such as a display specifically in the ward), or too wide (but the aim may be a specific group within the hospital). These issues will influence the type of material that will be most appropriate and, therefore, most effective.

Other issues to consider are:

- how long the display will be in use. If it is for a relatively long time, it could be worthwhile investing in more expensive materials so that they will last longer. For example, laminated paper or card will endure longer than normal paper;
- the layout of the display. Is it eyecatching? Does it draw people in and encourage them to read, or does it look boring and uninteresting?
- developing a critical eye. Look at other posters and displays. What attracts you to them? What puts you off?
- is the print large enough? Can it be read from a distance? Important points can be emphasised by enlarging the print;
- colour, pictures, photographs and drawings, which all make a display look more interesting;
- whether the poster or display will 'stand alone'. There could be details of people whom the reader could contact for more information, advice or support. It is a good idea to have some leaflets that people can take away. These can then support the material in the poster by acting as a reminder and offer new information. Likewise, posters can be an effective way of encouraging people to read leaflets;
- whether the material encourages people to think. This can be by asking questions, challenging attitudes or challenging behaviour;
- the amount of written material. A few well-chosen words will have more impact than reams of small print. People are more likely to read the material if there is less of it, particularly if they are in a hurry.

EXAMPLE OF A HOSPITAL-WIDE HEALTH PROMOTION INTERVENTION

A nurse employed as a hospital-based health promotion facilitator decided to increase awareness of the effects of alcohol for people in the hospital, whether staff, patients or visitors. She decided to set up a display in the main corridor of the hospital, so as to be as eyecatching as possible. The display was chosen to coincide with national 'Drinkwise Day', to gain maximum interest and publicity. An advertisement was inserted into the hospital newsletter, together with posters around the hospital site. The following month's newsletter included the results of the incorporated quiz, together with the name of the winner. The nurse planned the display to include:

- the title 'No or low alcohol?', to cover those people who should not drink any alcohol as well as those who needed to be aware of safe drinking levels;
- someone with knowledge of alcohol lifestyle issues to answer questions;

'No or Low' Quiz

1. Which is more fattening, an average portion of ice cream or a large gin and tonic?

2. Which of these statements are true?
   a. Alcohol increases heat loss from the body.
   b. Alcohol affects your sense of balance.
   c. Alcohol increases your ability to cope with pain.

3. What are the official recommended unit limits per week for alcohol consumption:
   a. For men.
   b. For women.
   c. Do these apply to all adults?

4. Which will help to sober you up most quickly?
   a. Black coffee.
   b. Fresh air.
   c. Cold shower.
   d. None of these.

5. How many hospital admissions are linked with alcohol?
   a. 1 in 500
   b. 1 in 50
   c. 1 in 5

6. Most drink/driving offences occur around Christmas and New Year. True or false?

   Tiebreaker Complete the following sentence in no more than 20 words: **The best way to say 'no' when offered a drink is to say**

   . . . .

   . . . .

   . . . .

Fig. 3 'No or Low' alcohol quiz

- posters with information about safe alcohol limits;
- posters about the consequences of alcohol, for example drinking and driving;
- samples of low alcohol drinks and non-alcoholic cocktails for people to try, together with some recipes;
- a variety of leaflets relating to alcohol consumption to meet different needs;
- a quiz (Figure 3) for people to assess their knowledge and to encourage them to look at the display. A small prize was offered for the winner of the quiz, (the answers to which are provided at the end of this chapter).

The display therefore offered:

- someone to talk to;
- things to do;
- written information;
- leaflets to take away.

Aim
To encourage all patients admitted with vascular disease who smoke to stop smoking.

Objective
All patients admitted with vascular disease who smoke will have an understanding of smoking and its effects on their health prior to discharge.

Action
1. Patients will have their smoking status and attitude to smoking assessed and recorded in their care plan on admission.
2. The primary nurse will discuss the effects of smoking with the patient.
3. Patients will receive written information as a back-up to verbal information.
4. A display about smoking will be mounted in the ward by July 25th.

Action Evaluation
1. Audit of all care plans over a 2-week period.
2. Interview with a sample of 20 patients to ascertain whether smoking has been discussed since admission.
3. Questionnaire, over a 2-week period, to all patients who smoke, asking about leaflets.
4. Look and see whether there is a display about smoking mounted in the ward by July 25th.

Fig. 4 Example of a ward-based health promotion strategy.

EXAMPLE OF A WARD-BASED HEALTH PROMOTION INTERVENTION

A health promotion strategy by hospital ward nurses could look like that in Figure 4.

EXAMPLE OF A STRATEGY LINKING THE HOSPITAL WITH THE COMMUNITY

Hospital staff felt that they should take wider responsibility for the health of the people who lived in the locality that the hospital served. They decided to target smoking and developed a programme of activities highlighting smoking, together with strategies to reach current smokers. To achieve this, they decided to:

- implement a 'No smoking' policy in the hospital;
- produce posters in the hospital highlighting the dangers of smoking;
- raise awareness by publishing articles in the local paper and giving talks in schools and to clubs and societies;
- use the local radio station to educate people about the risks of smoking and the services that the hospital offered;
- provide smoking cessation support for staff and patients, which would be offered to the local community. These included a telephone help line and a support group.

Although this is an ambitious range of services, the chances of success are much higher through targeting one topic in many ways, than from a piecemeal approach.

EXAMPLE OF A PLANNING STRATEGY

An acute surgical ward decided to identify 12 health promotion topics and then target one each month for the staff and patients on their ward. They developed a 'wheel' depicting each month of the year, together with the chosen topic for that month. From this, staff chose a topic to specialise in and could prepare in advance. They were careful to select topics to fit in with national campaigns, for example, 'No smoking day'.

ANSWERS TO THE 'NO OR LOW' QUIZ (FIGURE 3)

1. They contain approximately the same number of calories.
2. All are correct.
3. a. 21 units per week for men.
   b. 14 units per week for women.

c. No. Alcohol should be avoided by those with liver disease and in pregnancy, and is contraindicated with certain drugs.
4. d. None of these. Only time will effect the sobering-up process.
5. c. 1 in 5 hospital admissions are linked with alcohol.
6. False. Drinking and driving is a problem all year round. The peak time for offences tends to be in the early summer rather than at Christmas.

Part Two

Health Promotion Information

3

Smoking

SMOKING AND SOCIETY

Smoking not only affects individuals but also has large impacts on society, both negative:

- smoking causes around 100 000 deaths every year in the UK;
- one in four smokers dies before reaching 65 years of age;
- 50 million working days are lost every year from absenteeism resulting from smoking-related illness;
- cigarettes and other smoking materials account for 40% of all deaths from fire;

and positive:

- tobacco is the Government's third largest source of consumer revenue.

INCIDENCE AND TRENDS OF SMOKING

There are about 13.5 million smokers in the UK. Although the proportion of smokers to non-smokers has been steadily declining since the 1970s, there have been increases among women and also within the 16–24 age group.

HEALTH RISKS OF SMOKING

Tobacco smoke contains over 4000 different chemicals, of which 60 are known to be carcinogenic. The principal health risks come from nicotine, carbon monoxide and tar.

31

Nicotine

Nicotine is an alkali found in the moisture of the tobacco leaf. It forms minute droplets in smoke and is quickly absorbed into the body once inhaled. On inhalation, nicotine:

- increases the heart rate;
- raises blood pressure;
- increases hormone production;
- restricts peripheral blood flow;
- raises blood sugar levels;
- relaxes peripheral muscle.

Carbon monoxide

Carbon monoxide is found in high concentrations in tobacco smoke. It combines with haemoglobin to form carboxyhaemoglobin, reducing the level of oxygen in the blood. To compensate for oxygen depletion, the heart rate increases.

Carbon monoxide is particularly harmful during pregnancy, when it reduces the supply of oxygen to the uterus and developing foetus.

Tar

Seventy per cent of the tar in tobacco smoke condenses upon inhalation and is deposited in the lungs. Tar affects the lungs by:

- narrowing the bronchioles;
- increasing the secretion of bronchial mucus;
- damaging the small hairs that protect the lungs from dirt and infection (ciliostasis).

DISEASES ATTRIBUTED TO SMOKING

The three most common causes of smoking-related death are cancer, cardiovascular disease and chronic obstructive pulmonary disease.

Cancer

One third of all deaths from cancer can be attributed to smoking. Lung cancer kills around 40 000 people annually, 90% of whom are smokers.

Risk increases in proportion to the length of time a person has smoked. For example, doubling the length of time smoked from 10 to 20 years, with constant consumption levels, increases the chance of lung cancer

16-fold. The risk of lung cancer also increases steeply with age. The risk of lung cancer is, however, reversible. After 10 to 15 years of not smoking, the risk to an ex-smoker is only slightly greater than that to a person who has never smoked.

The risk of developing oral, laryngeal or oesophageal cancer increases with the number of cigarettes smoked. Alcohol has a significant effect on the risk of smokers developing these cancers. For example, a person who smokes more than 40 cigarettes per day and who drinks more than four units of alcohol per day increases the risk of oral and pharyngeal cancer by 35 times. Ninety per cent of all laryngeal cancers occur in people who smoke and drink excessive alcohol; 75% of all oral and pharyngeal cancers also occur in this group.

The risk of developing pancreatic cancer increases five-fold in those who smoke more than 20 cigarettes per day. However, the risk reduces to that of a non-smoker 10 years after stopping smoking.

The increased risk of bladder cancer has been found to be between 40% for female smokers and 70% for male smokers, compared to non-smokers.

The risk of leukaemia has also been found to be 53% higher for current smokers and 39% higher for ex-smokers than for non-smokers.

Cardiovascular disease

Cigarette smoking, raised cholesterol and hypertension are the three most firmly established non-hereditary risk factors leading to coronary heart disease. The risk of fatal coronary heart disease is 2.5 times higher in smokers than in non-smokers. Where these three non-hereditary factors are present, the risk of coronary heart disease is eight times higher than in non-smokers. Eighty-nine per cent of myocardial infarctions in men under 45 years old are attributed to cigarette smoking.

Smoking raises blood cholesterol levels. It also raises fibrinogen levels and platelet counts, making the blood more viscous. Combined with reduced oxygen in the blood from carbon monoxide, these factors increase the risk of atherosclerotic disease. Risk of angina and intermittent claudication also rise. Over time, there is a greater likelihood of thrombosis, potentially leading to myocardial infarction, stroke, aortic and other aneurysms and peripheral vasular disease, the latter accounting for the majority of the 2000 amputations yearly in England. Smokers account for 90% of people with symptoms of arterial disease of the legs, and thromboangiitis obliterans (Buerger's disease) is nearly always due to heavy cigarette smoking.

Chronic obstructive pulmonary disease

In 1989, bronchitis and emphysema accounted for 26 723 deaths in England, of which 90% were smoking related.

Younger smokers who give up smoking can expect their lung function to improve, but damage is unlikely to be reversible in older people. However, cessation of smoking will slow further deterioration.

Other diseases and disorders

Subarachnoid haemorrhage is more common in smokers, particularly for women who take the contraceptive pill.

Smokers have a higher incidence of stomach and duodenal ulcers than non-smokers, the lesions also taking longer to heal.

There is a higher incidence of dental caries and plaque in smokers. Smoking is also associated with the prevalence of oral leukoplakia and erythroplasia, premalignant conditions with the potential to lead to oral cancer.

Smoking increases the incidence of common conditions such as coughs, colds and influenza.

SMOKING AND WOMEN

Apart from the risks already discussed, there are other issues relevant to women who smoke. Fertility is reduced to 72% of that for non-smoking women, and smokers are more than three times as likely to take more than one year to conceive than are non-smokers.

Cigarette smoking is a risk factor for cervical cancer due to the decrease in the number of Langerhan's cells, which form part of the immune system. As there is a relationship between cell count and the number of cigarettes smoked, the risk increases over time.

On average, the menopause occurs two or three years earlier in smokers than non-smokers. The reduction in bone density associated with the menopause is also greater, resulting in an increased risk of osteoporosis.

SMOKING IN PREGNANCY

Smoking in pregnancy leads to increased risks for the mother:

- there is a higher risk of complications of pregnancy, for example bleeding, premature detachment of the placenta and premature rupture of the membranes;
- smoking more than 20 cigarettes per day almost doubles the risk of spontaneous abortion;

and for the foetus or baby:

- nicotine and carbon monoxide in the mother's body reduces the oxygen supply reaching the uterus and foetus via the placenta;
- growth is restricted. Babies of maternal smokers are on average 200 g lighter than those of comparable non-smoking mothers;
- perinatal mortality increases 35% where the mother smokes more than 20 cigarettes per day, and 20% for those who smoke fewer than this;
- smoking introduces cotinine, a nicotine derivative, into breast milk and may contribute to inadequate milk production;
- long-term physical growth may be affected;
- later intellectual development has been found to be imparied, for example in reading and mathematics in 16-year-olds and in the level of qualification of 23-year-olds.

PASSIVE SMOKING

Passive smoking is the inhalation of other people's tobacco smoke. The smoke may be categorised as either mainstream smoke (smoke exhaled by the smoker) or sidestream smoke (that rising from the end of a cigarette, pipe or cigar). In a room where people are smoking, 85% of the smoke in the air will be sidestream smoke, which is subsequently inhaled by others without the benefit of any filtering device. Several hundred annual deaths from lung cancer can be attributed to passive smoking. Likewise, prolonged exposure to tobacco smoke of people with pre-existing cardiac or respiratory conditions increases the risk of morbidity and mortality.

In homes where parents and others smoke, babies and children have been found to have cotinine levels equivalent to the consumption of 80 cigarettes per year. Passively smoking children are more prone to infections of the ear, nose and throat and are also more susceptible to serious chest infections, such as bronchitis and pneumonia. Similarly, the risk of respiratory diseases in the first year of life is significantly higher in the children of smokers than in those of non-smokers.

THE PHYSIOLOGICAL EFFECT OF SMOKING

Nicotine is a habit-forming drug, causing addiction in a similar way to heroin or cocaine. Nicotine craving occurs when there is a reduction in the nicotine level from the established normal for a person. Thus, giving up smoking is not easy, as the person will suffer craving and physical withdrawal symptoms. The effect of smoking is rapid, so craving is quickly diminished through smoking. Nicotine's effect on the brain begins only seven to eight seconds after inhalation.

THE PSYCHOLOGICAL EFFECT OF SMOKING

The effects of nicotine on mood and behaviour are complex. Key factors are the length of time someone has been smoking, the number of cigarettes smoked daily, how deeply the smoke is inhaled and the time and place in which smoking takes place.

Despite the detrimental effects on physical health, smokers often enjoy smoking. It becomes part of their outward character and can be a coping strategy. Smoking encourages psychological dependence by providing a prop or form of comfort.

THE SOCIAL EFFECT OF SMOKING

Peer pressure can be a strong influence on smoking behaviour, smoking being the acceptable norm for a particular group of people. Here, it may not only be acceptable but also expected or required for full 'membership' of the group.

Although smokers have been in the minority in the population since 1976, and smoking is banned in many workplaces, places of entertainment and transport systems, public smoking is still widespread.

Alcohol is a major trigger for smokers, especially within a social context, such as a party or pub.

THE HEALTHIER ALTERNATIVE

Giving up smoking is the single most effective way in which smokers can improve their health. Physically, benefits can be detected after a few weeks as the body begins to repair the damage done by smoking.

Psychologically, giving up smoking can:

- reduce the anxiety felt about health;
- increase self-confidence by demonstrating control over one's lifestyle.

STRATEGIES FOR GIVING UP SMOKING

However much support someone may get from family, friends, colleagues and health-care professionals, giving up remains a personal decision that smokers have to reach for themselves.

There are many strategies and supports available, the most important being the ones that the person perceives to be of the most help to them personally. The following stratgegies have been found to aid giving up.

Planning a programme

- Start a smoking diary, noting the times and circumstances when cigarettes are smoked. Make a note of the times when smoking is felt to be most needed and when it is least needed. These will show the individual patterns of smoking and thus the times and situations that the person will find easiest and hardest.
- Record how much money is spent on smoking. This can help to strengthen resolve, as people may be surprised by how much their habit costs.
- Decide on a firm date for giving up. Linking this to a particular event can help to increase commitment and also provide distraction.
- Enlist the support of family, friends and colleagues by telling them of the intention to stop smoking on a particular date. Ask them not to offer cigarettes.
- Decide on something to buy, and determine the date on which it can be bought, based on its cost and how much is spent on cigarettes.
- On the date to give up, throw away all smoking materials, including cigarettes, matches, lighters and ashtrays, and do something special to mark the occasion.
- Using information gained from the smoking diary, change routines over the first few days so as to avoid situations that trigger smoking. If they cannot be avoided, plan alternative activities in advance.
- Take each day at a time. Do not worry about not smoking tomorrow.
- Learn to resist temptation from others. One single cigarette *does* count, as resolve is broken, which can easily lead to another and another cigarette.
- Remember the reason for giving up.
- Count the days towards buying the treat, then go out and buy it.

Nicotine substitutes

Withdrawal from nicotine dependence is a major part of the discomfort felt when stopping smoking. Nicotine substitutes have been developed to help alleviate this by replacing tobacco as the agent of nicotine delivery to the body and freeing the smoker from the habitual behaviour patterns associated with smoking. They should be used instead of smoking, rather than while smoking.

- Nicotine gum should be chewed gently and slowly over about 20–30 minutes. If chewed too fast, it tastes bitter. Gum is available in strengths of 2 mg and 4 mg per piece, the latter only on prescription. Users of the gum are advised to stop if the taste is too strong and if they become light-headed or suffer hiccoughs.

- Nicotine patches deliver the nicotine transdermally, and are available both with and without prescription. Packs contain patches of varying strengths. Users start with the strongest patches and then follow a course of patches of diminishing strength. Each patch lasts for 16–24 hours. It is inadvisable to time a patch change for first thing in the morning as withdrawal symptoms may be experienced on waking, which can be distressing.

BARRIERS TO BEING HEALTHIER

Changing from cigarettes to cigars or a pipe

Smoking-associated mortality rates in this group are higher than in non-smokers, although lower than for smokers. This is because these smokers do not tend to inhale as much as cigarette smokers. However, cigar and pipe smoke is at least as, and may be more, carcinogenic than cigarette smoke.

Ex-cigarette smokers who smoke five cigars per day have a four-fold risk of myocardial infarction compared to smokers who have given up smoking completely.

Changing to low tar cigarettes

The advantage of changing to a lower tar cigarette is often lost through smoking more cigarettes per day and/or inhaling more deeply. This can easily happen as the perceived risks of smoking are seen to be less and as the smoker tries to achieve the same effect as with the previous higher tar cigarettes.

Changing to herbal cigarettes

Smoking herbal cigarettes reinforces the smoking behaviour pattern. They may not contain nicotine but still produce carbon monoxide and tar, some brands having a tar content equivalent to middle or high tar cigarettes.

Changing to smokeless tobacco

Tobacco that can be chewed, inhaled or sucked has also been shown to be carcinogenic. Studies in the USA and India have detected high risks of cancer of the oral cavity, pharynx, larynx and oesophagus.

Withdrawal effects

The physiological symptoms of withdrawal do not tend to last long, most being gone within 15–20 days. On giving up smoking, some of the following symptoms may be experienced, although few smokers experience them all:

- dizziness and light-headedness, as the body adapts to new oxygen levels in the blood following carbon monoxide reduction. This may last a few days;
- headaches, due to a reduction in blood pressure. This may last about three days;
- tingling sensations, aches and pains in the muscles, sweating hands and trembling, which may last for two weeks;
- altered bowel patterns and nausea, as nicotine by-products are excreted and not replaced. This may last up to four days;
- sleep disturbance and vivid dreams. Normal patterns should be re-established within two weeks;
- coughing, as bronchial cilia begin to recover and expel tar and mucus from the lungs. Coughing may last up to three weeks.

STAYING AN EX-SMOKER

Long after the physiological symptoms of withdrawal have faded away, there may still be the psychological urge to smoke. The smoking diary can act as a reminder of why the person decided to stop smoking.

Appetite tends to increase after stopping smoking, but this can be counteracted by encouraging low calorie snacks and taking more exercise.

Ex-smokers are often irritable for the first few weeks. They should try to avoid confrontations with others and instead try to enlist their support.

HOSPITAL SMOKING POLICIES

Hospital authorities should be leading the way in establishing no-smoking policies. Unless health-care professionals can be seen to demonstrate good health practices, their health-care advice will lack credibility.

As employers, managers should recognise that smoking:

- is a serious health risk to their employees;
- increases staff absence due to sickness;
- reduces staff efficiency;
- is a significant cause of fires in public buildings.

No smoking policies offer two broad options: a complete ban on smoking on the premises or allowing smoking only in designated areas.

A complete ban on smoking

This can be difficult to enforce and needs the cooperation of staff in complying. Ethical issues need to be debated by the staff, and patients' views sought. For example, when a nurse has just told a person that their spouse has died, is it an appropriate time to refuse the relative a cigarette when smoking may have been a coping strategy for many years? Unless such issues are discussed, there may be discontent and resentment among the staff.

Hospital staff may resent not being allowed to smoke when off duty but still on the premises, for example at meal times. This can lead to clusters of uniformed staff hovering around the main entrance of the hospital.

A complete ban on smoking should not, therefore, be considered as the total solution to the problems of smoking in hospital. Opportunities should be created for all those whom the policy would affect to discuss the implications. This should involve staff, patients, visitors and also members of the local community, as they, too, may enter the premises in the future as patients or visitors.

As giving up smoking is not easy, support should be offered to those who decide to stop. This could involve the setting up of mutual support groups or sessions offering alternative coping strategies, such as relaxation classes.

A partial ban on smoking

This, too, may not be an easy option. Where will smoking be allowed, and who can smoke there? For example, if an area is designated for patient smoking, how will dependent patients get to it? As this involves nurses' time in taking patients or staying with them, ethical issues arise that need to be discussed.

For staff, key issues are where will they smoke and will it affect others, either as passive smoking for other staff or by patients having to come in contact with staff who smell of smoke.

There are two options for the place to smoke: a smoking room, which is an area enclosed by solid floor-to-ceiling partitions, or a smoking area, which may simply be part of a larger space with only limited physical separation. Although provision of smoking and non-smoking areas in the same room will reduce peak exposure concentrations for non-smokers, this alone is not effective in reducing overall exposure to tobacco smoke.

Smoking rooms have the disadvantage of using up space that could be used for health-care and related activities. They also cost money as part of the hospital premises, and need extra resources for more frequent decorating, replacement of furnishings and additional ventilation. Often, the television room or dayroom has become the designated area for smoking on a ward, which then excludes non-smokers if they wish, for personal or health reasons to avoid smoke.

4

Alcohol

Alcohol is probably the most acceptable drug in the UK, nine out of ten adults claiming to drink it. Yet, it has a highly detrimental effect on individuals, families and society.

Alcohol has been found to contribute to accidents and absenteeism from work: between 8 and 14 million working days are thought to be lost annually from alcohol drinking. People with alcohol problems consult their general practitioner nearly twice as often as the average patient, and heavy drinkers tend to be high users of hospital services. It is estimated that approximately 25% of male in-patients have either a current or a previous alcohol problem.

Alcohol not only affects the person who drinks it but also those with whom the drinker comes into contact and society in general. Alcohol misuse is associated with:

- 60% of attempted suicides;
- 30% of divorces;
- 40% of incidents of domestic violence;
- 20% of cases of child abuse;
- 35% of all domestic accidents;
- 40% of deaths in fires.

INCIDENCE AND TRENDS OF ALCOHOL MISUSE

In 1989, 92 820 people in the UK were convicted of, or cautioned for, drunkenness offences. Although the number of drink–drive fatalities has decreased over the past 10 years, alcohol is still implicated in the cause of 15% of deaths from road traffic accidents. In 1990, 800 people

42

died and 20 100 people were injured in the UK as a result of drink-related accidents.

Cultural issues may mean that certain groups, such as Asian women, will deny drinking alcohol. Other groups may develop different patterns of drinking alcohol, for example drinking alone or consuming large quantities of alcohol in a short period of time.

Currently, approximately 28% of men and 11% of women in the UK drink in excess of 'sensible limits'. Seven per cent of men drink over 51 units per week, while 2% of women consume in excess of 36 units per week. For both sexes, younger people tend to have the highest consumption levels. Fourteen per cent of professional women usually drink more than 14 units per week, compared with 6% of women in lower socioeconomic groups. There is little difference in men's drinking levels by socioeconomic group. Although most people appear to know about recommended limits, research shows that only a small minority were able to give the correct limits for their sex.

Asians over the age of 40 are likely to drink more alcohol than younger Asians, yet it is the other way around for white men. Afro-Caribbean and white children are more likely to have tried alcohol than Asian children and are also more likely to be regular drinkers of alcohol.

DEFINING ALCOHOL CONSUMPTION

'Sensible drinking' is defined as:

- up to 21 units per week for men, spread throughout the week, with one or two alcohol-free days;
- up to 14 units per week for women, spread throughout the week, and also with one or two alcohol-free days.

A unit is defined as 8 g or 10 ml of alcohol, which, in terms of actual drinks, equals:

- one half pint of ordinary strength (3–4%) beer, lager or cider;
- one single measure of spirits (25 ml or 1/6th gill);
- one small glass of wine (95 ml or 3 fl oz);
- one measure of vermouth or aperitif (50 ml or ⅓rd gill).

Women are advised to drink less alcohol than men because:

- they experience higher peak plasma concentrations of alcohol;
- they have more subcutaneous fat (which stores alcohol) than men;
- they have lower levels of alcohol dehydrogenase, the enzyme responsible for the metabolism of alcohol;

- liver disorders, obesity, malnutrition and gastrointestinal haemorrhage appear to develop earlier in women and at lower levels of
alcohol consumption than for men.

HEALTH RISKS OF ALCOHOL CONSUMPTION

Accidental injury

After drinking two units of alcohol, the risk of accidental injury starts to
increase. After five units, the risk of an accident is doubled, and after 10
units, the risk is 10 times more. Loss of consciousness, dysarthria and
ataxia can occur after 10–12 units, while more than 25 units can be fatal.

Nutrition

Alcohol stops the body absorbing and using vitamins, particularly
thiamine, other group B vitamins and vitamin C. Malnutrition is often
linked to heavy drinking due to a poor diet, combined with impaired
intestinal function and absorption.

Chronic diseases

Alcohol interacts with many drugs, so people taking regular medication,
for example for diabetes, epilepsy, ulcers and hypertension, are at high
risk of complications from drug interaction.

DISEASES ATTRIBUTED TO ALCOHOL

Chronic liver disease

Liver damage is common in those drinking excessive amounts of alcohol.
It can include hepatitis, cirrhosis and primary hepatocellular carcinoma.
Between 10% and 30% of excessive drinkers will develop irreversible
cirrhosis, where normal liver tissue is replaced by fibrous tissue. Liver
function becomes severely impaired and life expectancy is reduced. Death
from liver disease is 10 times higher in heavy drinkers than in non-drinkers.

Cancer

Alcohol increases the risk of developing cancer in all parts of the
gastrointestinal tract:

- Primary liver cancer develops in approximately 8% of people with
alcoholic cirrhosis of the liver.

- Non-smoking heavy drinkers have more than twice the risk of developing cancers of the oral cavity, pharynx and oesophagus than do non-drinkers.
- There is an increased risk of colorectal cancers. Beer in particular is associated with rectal cancer, as it contains significant levels of N-nitrosamines, which are carcinogenic.

Risks of cancer are also higher in other body systems:

- Non-smoking heavy drinkers have four times the risk of developing cancer of the larynx than non-drinkers.
- Some studies have suggested an association between cancer of the breast and alcohol consumption as low as 14 units per week.

Cardiovascular disease

High alcohol intake is associated with a two to four times greater risk of stroke. Vasoconstriction of cerebral blood vessels is thought to account for the association between high alcohol intake over short periods of time and stroke.

Excess alcohol is probably the most common identifiable cause of hypertension. There is a linear relationship between alcohol consumption and blood pressure for most people, independent of age, weight and cigarette smoking: the more alcohol that is consumed, the higher the blood pressure will become.

Moderate amounts of alcohol are considered to provide a protective effect against cardiovascular disease, because of an increase in the concentration of high density lipoprotein cholesterol, associated with a reduced risk of coronary heart disease.

ALCOHOL AND PREGNANCY

Alcohol at conception and in pregnancy leads to increased risks for the developing foetus or baby:

- Alcohol lowers the sperm count in men, reducing the chance of conception.
- There is an increased incidence of mid-trimester abortions, still-births, congenital retardation and delayed physical and mental development.
- Drinking more than 10 units per week can lead to a low birth weight.
- Heavy drinking can result in foetal alcohol syndrome, a

combination of developmental delay, growth retardation, neurological abnormalities and facial dysmorphology.

ALCOHOL AND SMOKING

Alcohol and smoking combined represent a greater risk to health than the sum of the individual risks. The chance of developing oesophageal cancer is 150 times greater for smokers who drink heavily than for those who do neither. There is also a significant increase of chronic bronchitis and emphysema in those who both drink heavily and smoke.

ALCOHOL AND OBESITY

The high calorific content of alcohol can contribute to obesity for many drinkers. When used as an alternative to food, a poor diet results, as alcohol lacks many vitamins, proteins and other essential nutrients.

DEPENDENCE

Anyone who finds it difficult to stop drinking alcohol has some degree of dependence.

Physical dependence is the need for alcohol in order to prevent withdrawal symptoms. The body develops a tolerance to alcohol, and withdrawal symptoms will occur if the alcohol level is reduced.

Psychological dependence is the felt need for alcohol in order to achieve an effect, for example pleasure or the ability to cope with a situation. This is the most common type of dependence and probably the most difficult to overcome.

THE PHYSIOLOGICAL EFFECT OF ALCOHOL

Alcohol is a depressant. Once swallowed, it takes less than five minutes for the brain to be affected. Brain activity becomes slower, balance is impaired and the alcohol acts as an anaesthetic. Heat loss is increased due to increased peripheral circulation.

The highest concentrations of alcohol occur in the liver, as blood reaches the liver directly from the stomach via the portal vein. Most alcohol is metabolised by the liver, only 2–4% being excreted unchanged via the respiratory tract and kidneys. Metabolic abnormalities can occur from the oxidation of excess alcohol, including over-production of lactic acid and ketones, uric acid retention, hyperlipidaemia and accumulation of fat in the liver.

The rate of absorption depends on other stomach contents and the concentration of the alcohol in the drink. Blood alcohol levels also depend on sex, weight, previous exposure to alcohol and the use of other drugs.

Alcohol is metabolised at a rate of about one unit per hour in healthy adults, starting about 20 minutes after the first drink. In patients with liver damage, alcohol is present for much longer; for example, the consumption of six units will still give rise to detectable levels of blood alcohol 24 hours later.

Alcohol reacts with other drugs, making some, for example some antibiotics, less effective and increasing the effects of others, such as sedatives.

THE PSYCHOLOGICAL EFFECT OF ALCOHOL

Problems relating to intoxication include:

- insomnia;
- depression;
- suicide;
- amnesia;
- anxiety;
- attempted suicide.

Problems relating to regular heavy drinking include the above plus:

- personality changes;
- delirium tremens;
- withdrawal fits;
- hallucinations;
- dementia;
- drug misuse.

THE SOCIAL EFFECT OF ALCOHOL

Alcohol has an effect from an early age; 89% of 9 to 15-year-olds have had their first alcoholic drink by the age of 13. The most common setting is in the home, where 10% drink at least once a week with their parents. Drinking behaviour is associated with parental behaviour and attitudes, peer group influence and family relationships and conflict.

Alcohol lessens inhibitions and encourages risk-taking, for example unprotected sex, which increases the risk of HIV, other infections and unwanted pregnancies.

IDENTIFYING WHEN SOMEONE HAS AN ALCOHOL PROBLEM

Personal signs and symptoms

Apart from pathology related to excess alcohol consumption, there are other features that could indicate that someone either has, or is on the way to developing, an alcohol problem:

- Drunkenness.
- The breath frequently smells of alcohol.
- The breath frequently smells of something strong, for example, peppermints; this may be to try to mask the smell of alcohol.
- Recurrent gastrointestinal disturbance.
- Evidence of frequent minor accidents, for example bruises, cigarette burns and abrasions, and reports of accidents.
- Anaemia or malnutrition.
- Peripheral neuritis.
- A history of frequent visits to the general practitioner for other reasons, for example sleeping difficulties and tiredness.
- Signs of mental health problems, for example forgetfulness, fatigue, lethargy, anxiety, mild depression and unexplained mood changes.
- Signs apparent in family members, for example emotional or behavioural disturbance and signs of abuse or neglect of children.

High risk groups

As well as individual factors leading to alcohol problems, there are also specific groups who are at a higher risk of developing difficulties. These comprise:

- those in stress occupations;
- those in occupations such as in hotel and bar work where alcohol is easily accessible;
- those in occupations where a lot of time is spent in isolation, for example travelling sales staff;
- people who are in temporary accommodation or hostels;
- people who have family members with an alcohol problem;
- those whose social life focuses on environments such as clubs and bars, where alcohol is consumed.

Alcohol meters

Alcohol meters measure the ethanol concentration in air expelled from the lungs. They are of limited use in the medical setting and are most frequently used by the police to detect drivers who have consumed alcohol at levels above the legal limit for driving. Such tests may provide useful information if other features suggest alcohol abuse.

STRATEGIES FOR LIMITING ALCOHOL CONSUMPTION

Some of these strategies may be inappropriate for those who need to stop drinking alcohol totally, for example where there is pathological change from excess alcohol or where some drugs are contraindicated.

Planning a programme

- Start a drinking diary, noting the times and circumstances when drinking occurs. This demonstrates individual habits and can be used to indicate situations to avoid or when to plan alternatives.
- Record how much money is spent on alcohol. Being aware of cost can strengthen determination to cut down, particularly if attractive alternatives are found for the money.
- Set realistic and achievable limits. Two limits might be useful, one for normal everyday life and one for special occasions.
- Make each drink last longer by taking smaller sips, putting the glass down between sips and increasing the time between drinks.
- Find a distraction. This could be a new hobby or a distraction in the social situation, for example playing darts or pool rather than just standing by the bar.
- Try other drinks. Change to a low alcohol or non-alcoholic alternative.
- Dilute spirits so that it takes longer to drink the alcohol.
- Eat as well as drinking. Food before or during drinking slows down the absorption of alcohol into the bloodstream and also provides a distraction.
- Measure the alcohol in drinks realistically. When pouring drinks at home it is easy to pour volumes larger than pub measures.
- Delay the first drink until later in the day. Set limits on the time, which can then be altered over a period to reduce the amount of available drinking time.
- Establish alcohol-free days each week. It is important not to drink more on the other days to 'compensate'.
- Ideally, say 'No'. This can be practised beforehand, as it is often found to be harder than perceived.
- Buy a treat with the money saved from drinking less.

Projecting a healthy attitude towards alcohol

Events in the hospital, such as leaving parties and fundraising events, can be used to project a healthy attitude towards alcohol. A good supply and wide range of low alcohol and alcohol-free drinks should be available. It is crucial that this attitude towards alcohol is shared, and seen to be shared, by staff at all levels.

General alcohol awareness can be raised throughout the hospital by exhibitions, quizzes, tasting sessions of low alcohol and non-alcoholic drinks and leaflets. These should be backed up with the offer of confidential support and help for those who need it, either because they themselves have an alcohol problem or because they are closely associated with someone who does.

HOSPITAL POLICIES ON ALCOHOL

One in five accidents at work involves alcohol. One in ten employees in a hospital is likely to have an alcohol problem, which means that in every area of the hospital, there is likely to be at least one staff member with a problem concerning alcohol.

Alcohol is associated with many professional difficulties in hospitals, for example impaired judgement, poor relationships with staff and patients and unprofessional behaviour.

A unit policy on alcohol allows managers to:

- recognise signs of problem drinking;
- develop a strategy for helping and supporting individuals;
- prevent alcohol-related problems arising.

The alcohol policy should:

- demonstrate a sensitive attitude, identifying support and help for both health-care staff and patients;
- have rules about alcohol use in working hours in order to improve safety and good professional practice;
- make clear any disciplinary issues involved;
- establish communication links separating support from disciplinary actions, so as to enable people to ask for help without fear of disciplinary action;
- consider alcohol use that may not be covered by the usual rules, for example staff leaving parties and Christmas and fundraising events;
- consider use of alcohol outside the hospital. Support should be offered to staff so that they can receive help before a problem arises at work;
- start from a specific well-publicised date.

5

Nutrition

Unlike cigarettes and alcohol, we are all naturally dependent on food to survive: everyone needs to eat in some form or other. However, in many countries food has ceased to be only a necessity for physical survival and now plays an important role in psychological and social well-being. The type of food eaten, where it is consumed and with whom all make statements about the type of people we are and the social world that we live in.

Unfortunately, and incorrectly, many people seem to think that 'healthy eating' means giving up the foods that they enjoy, eating foods that they dislike and spending more money. It is up to health-care professionals to show them that this need not be the case. Healthy eating can be fun! It also need not be expensive.

INCIDENCE AND TRENDS IN NUTRITION

As a society, we are consuming increasing amounts of fast food and snacks and fewer family meals. This has physiological effects – increased consumption of salt, fat and sugar – and psychosocial effects – meals as a time of being together with family or friends are less common.

In the UK, many people increase their risk of coronary heart disease and stroke by the type of diet they eat – too much fat and salt and not enough fresh fruit and vegetables. In recent years, there has been a rise in the popularity of vegetarianism. There are different degrees of vegetarianism, ranging from not eating meat to not eating anything of animal origin (veganism). The more restricted the diet, the more thought that is required to balance nutrients. Vegetarian diets can be healthy but are not necessarily so: they can still be high in fat, sugar and salt.

However, it is not the type of diet that is important, but whether it is well balanced.

DISEASES AND CONDITIONS RELATED TO NUTRITION

Obesity

For the vast majority of obese people, obesity is primary, ie there is no predisposing pathological cause. Thus, the majority of people who are overweight consume too many calories in proportion to the amount of energy they expend or expend too few calories for the amount they consume. Those who are at risk from obesity are:

- people with an underlying disease process, such as an endocrinological disturbance;
- patients experiencing a sudden drop in activity levels, for example from bedrest following trauma. However, the metabolic rate initially rises as a response to trauma, so at this stage there are increased metabolic requirements;
- those who overeat for psychological reasons, for example comfort eaters who use food as a coping mechanism when faced with stress.

Obesity increases both morbidity and mortality from a number of disorders, including coronary heart disease, respiratory disease, diabetes and hypertension.

Coronary heart disease and stroke

Coronary heart disease and stroke are major health problems in the UK, and are responsible for more premature deaths than any other form of disease. They arise from a complex combination of many factors, some of which cannot be altered:

- genetic factors;
- race;
- sex;

and some of which can:

- smoking;
- inadequate levels of physical activity;
- obesity;
- hypertension;
- high serum cholesterol.

Although the debate about the relative importance of all these factors continues, obesity and hypertension are clearly indicated as predisposing factors and may both be modified through dietary change. These are discussed further in the section on 'Specific disorders with nutritional implications', page 66.

Anorexia and bulimia

Although these are two different conditions, individual patients often suffer from symptoms of both, and bulimia often develops after a period of anorexia-related symptoms.

Women suffer these disorders 10 times more often than men, often starting when they are teenagers. Anorexia usually starts with the type of 'normal' dieting that many teenagers do, but does not stop when an appropriate weight is reached. It is thought to affect about 1 in every 150 15-year-old girls. Although anorexia is literally defined as 'loss of appetite', sufferers actually have a normal appetite but exert great control over their eating.

Anorexia and bulimia can result from a variety of causes. These include:

- pressure from society. 'Thinness' is portrayed as desirable on television, in magazines and in films;
- as a way of gaining control over something. Teenage girls particularly may feel out of control as they develop physically, emotionally and psychologically. Dieting helps them to put some order and control back into their lives;
- as a way of delaying puberty and, therefore, the problems that are perceived to be involved with growing up;
- as a way to rebel against the family;
- as a reaction to an emotional event such as family break-up, in order to cope with unhappiness.

Signs and symptoms of anorexia include:

- fear of being fat;
- undereating;
- excessive weight loss;
- increased and abnormal levels of exercise;
- amenorrhoea;
- excessive quantities of fruit and vegetables being eaten, as they are low calorie but filling foods.

As time progresses, bulimia may develop in a greater effort to reduce weight, although it may also develop without a history of anorexia. It is thought to affect about three out of every 100 females at some time in their life, often those between the ages of 20 and 25 who have been overweight as children. Signs and symptoms of bulimia include:

- a possible history of anorexia;
- fear of being fat;
- binge eating. This is eating large amounts of fattening foods in a short period of time;
- irregular menstruation;
- induced vomiting;
- excessive use of laxatives,
- normal weight, as a combination of bingeing and vomiting can result in an acceptable number of calories.

The physiological effects of anorexia and bulimia can include:

- constipation and damage to bowel muscles from excessive laxative use;
- muscle weakness and brittle bones as the diet lacks essential vitamins and minerals;
- enamel on the teeth dissolving in the stomach acid regurgitated during vomiting;
- a puffy face from swollen salivary glands;
- renal damage;
- epileptic fits;
- death, if the condition is not recognised and treated.

The psychological effects of anorexia and bulimia can include:

- disturbed sleep;
- depression;
- difficulty in concentrating.

THE PHYSIOLOGICAL EFFECT OF NUTRITION – THE HEALTHY DIET

A balanced diet is one that provides the right mixture of nutrients for the body to work efficiently and effectively. No single type of food contains all the necessary nutrients, so a selection of foods is needed to fulfil requirements. A useful way to consider the balance of a diet is to look at foods as belonging to four broad categories or groups:

- starchy foods;
- dairy products;

- meat, poultry, fish and meat alternatives;
- vegetables and fruit.

Some foods, such as cheese and potatoes, belong to more than one category.

The amount of food that should be eaten from each group depends on several factors:

- age;
- sex;
- levels of physical activity;
- existing weight.

Starchy foods, for example bread, cereals, pasta and potato, provide starch, fibre, vitamins and some iron. Wholegrain varieties are particularly healthy, as they contain most fibre.

Milk and milk products, including soya milks, provide calcium, B vitamins and some fat.

Meat and its vegetarian alternatives, such as tofu and quorn, provide protein, iron, B vitamins and some fat. Pulses, nuts and seeds provide protein, iron, B vitamins and fibre.

Fruit and vegetables provide vitamins A and C, fibre and some iron. Vitamins can be destroyed in cooking, but can be saved by cooking quickly with minimum amounts of water. Fruit and vegetables are low in calories, so are useful sources of nutrients for those following a weight-reducing diet.

Using the four food groups above helps to establish a healthier diet by allowing for a range of foods. The next stage is to get the right balance of fat, fibre, salt and sugar. Too much or too little of these can lead to an unhealthy diet, despite a variety of foods being eaten.

Fat

Fats are a concentrated source of energy and provide some vitamins, and thus a high fat diet is sometimes recommended by dietitians. However, excess fat can lead to heart disease and stroke by raising blood cholesterol and causing atherosclerosis.

There are three types of fat in food:

- *saturated fats*, found mainly in foods of animal origin, hard margarines and some oils. High intakes may cause a rise in the level of blood cholesterol, one of the factors linked to coronary heart disease;
- *monounsaturated fats*, found in dairy products, meat and olive oil. Scientists suggest that these may lower blood cholesterol levels;

- *polyunsaturated fats*, found in oily fish, nuts, sunflower and corn oils. Consumed in moderation, they appear to be beneficial in lowering the risk of myocardial infarction.

Cholesterol is a fatty substance essential for survival. It is naturally present in the body, being made from saturated fat by the liver, and is involved in the production of hormones and vitamin D. It is needed by body cells for metabolism and structural purposes. However, some people are thought to have too much cholesterol in their blood, either because of hereditory factors or because of a high cholesterol diet from eating too much saturated fat. Cholesterol is found in some foods (dietary cholesterol), but for most people this does not appear to have a major effect on the amount of cholesterol in the bloodstream.

Non-starch polysaccharides (fibre)

Non-starch polysaccharides (fibre) found in starchy food help to protect against haemorrhoids, diverticular disease, constipation, coronary heart disease, stroke and cancer of the bowel. Fibre is only found in foods derived from plants; there is none in animal products. Although bran is a potent source of fibre, it does not provide the other nutrients that can be found in other fibre-rich foods. Phytates in high fibre food can limit the absorption of some minerals.

Salt

About two-thirds of the salt present in the diet comes from processed foods and convenience foods, so can be difficult to detect, but information concerning this should be available on the label. Salt may appear on the label as 'sodium chloride' or 'monosodium glutamate'.

Although some salt is needed in the diet, most people consume too much for good health. The average intake is about two and a half teaspoons of salt per day, mainly in processed food, but only about half a teaspoonful is actually needed. Too much salt in the diet can lead to hypertension and can cause coronary heart disease, stroke and kidney disease.

Sugar

Sugar contains no nutrients, only calories. It can be a contributory factor to tooth decay, damage being greatest when sugar is in contact with the teeth for long periods of time, for example when sucking sweets. Sugar eaten during a meal causes less tooth decay, as it is washed off the teeth by other food and drinks; however, the calories are still consumed and may lead to a weight problem. Sugary foods may sometimes provide a useful source of calories for patients who have poor appetites.

Vitamins A, C and E

The 'ACE' vitamins are thought to help prevent coronary heart disease through protecting cholesterol in the blood vessels from damage. When cholesterol is damaged by free radicals in the blood, it is thought to be more likely to deposit on the vascular walls, leading to restricted arteries and, therefore, a greater risk of coronary heart disease. The ACE vitamins act by destroying the free radicals.

The uncontrolled action of free radicals in the blood is also thought to be one of the risk factors in cancer. By destroying the free radicals, the ACE vitamins protect cells from damage and, therefore, may help to protect against some types of cancer.

Additives

Food additives have recently been the target of much bad publicity. An E number given to an additive shows that it is recognised as safe by the European Community. Additives that are permitted in the UK are considered safe for almost the whole population; however, a few people may be allergic to a particular additive in the same way that others are allergic to particular foods. A number not prefixed by E means that the additive has been approved for use in the UK but has not been accepted by the European Community.

Additives are added to food to:

- enable it to be stored for longer;
- improve the flavour, for example monosodium glutamate (621);
- change the colour of the food;
- act as a substitute, for example saccharin or aspartame replacing sugar.

The types of additive are:

- *preservatives*, which protect against microorganisms that would lead to food poisoning. They help to reduce wastage and allow for a wider range of foods in the shops;
- *emulsifiers* and *stabilisers*, which enable oils and fats to mix with water to make the food smoother and creamier. Stabilisers prevent them from separating again;
- *antioxidants*, which stop fats and oils from becoming rancid and protect fat-soluble vitamins from oxidising;

- *colours*, which can alter or enhance the appearance of the food to make it look more attractive;
- *sweeteners*, which are either concentrated compared to sugar so only small quantities are needed (intense sweeteners) or have about the same sweetness as sugar (bulk sweeteners);
- other additives, which include anti-caking agents, flour improvers, anti-foaming agents, bulking agents and solvents.

THE PSYCHOLOGICAL EFFECT OF NUTRITION

Concern about weight may often mask psychological problems such as:

- negative body image;
- lack of self-confidence;
- stress.

These can lead to eating disorders such as:

- bingeing;
- bulimia;
- anorexia;
- overeating.

Some people may suffer one of these conditions, whereas others experience a combination.

THE SOCIAL AND CULTURAL EFFECTS OF NUTRITION

The type of food that is eaten, how it is cooked and when it is eaten depends on a variety of factors:

- tradition and habit;
- beliefs and attitudes about food and eating;
- childhood experiences;
- religious practices;
- the amount of money available, as determined by both income and the perceived importance of types of food compared with other items to be bought;
- moral decisions, for example for vegetarians who refuse to eat meat as an expressed choice, as a protest against the way in which animals are reared.

Any changes in diet will need to take these factors into account, otherwise they may be unacceptable to the patient who may not either change or sustain the initial change.

RELIGIOUS PRACTICES

Within any religion, there are many levels of conformity to expected practices by different individuals. Some people may be completely orthodox, following the rules exactly, whereas others may 'belong' to a particular religion in name only. It is, therefore, extremely important to discuss with the patient the effect of religion on their dietary needs. Sensitivity is often required, particularly if there is conflict between different family members.

Christianity

Christianity does not generally tend to influence dietary patterns. However, some Christians choose to fast at specific times or may restrict certain food, for example during Lent, the 40 days prior to Easter Day.

Hinduism

Many Hindus are vegetarian. Generally meat-eaters will not eat beef as the cow is regarded as sacred.

Days of fasting are common, but may follow different patterns, varying from no food being eaten for the day, to a day where foods eaten are restricted to those considered pure, for example rice and fruit.

The caste system dictates who can prepare and share food.

Islam

Food laws for Moslems are derived from their religious book, the Koran. The Koran forbids the consumption of alcohol, pork, carnivorous animals and some birds. Poultry and fish with scales are both permitted foods.

Any meat that is eaten needs to be from animals killed by ritual slaughter – Halal meat.

During the lunar month of Ramadan, Moslems fast between sunrise and sunset. However, those who are ill, pregnant or on a journey are excused, provided that the time missed is made up at another time. Despite this allowance, Moslems may find it difficult to accept that they are too ill to fast when the rest of the family are doing so.

Sikhism

Sikhism draws upon both Hindu and Moslem traditions. Vegetarianism is not uncommon, and Sikhs who eat meat will not eat beef or pork.

Judaism

Most devout Jews adhere to the Jewish Kashrut or dietary laws. They may not eat pork, pork products, shellfish or any fish without fins or scales, but may eat meat from any animal that has cloven hooves and chews cud. They are also permitted herbivorous birds. Any meat that is eaten needs to be from animals killed in a special way so as to be kosher.

Milk and meat may not be used together in cooking. Meat and milk products must be kept apart and different cooking utensils used for each.

Jews may fast for 24 hours at the feast of Yom Kippur, the Day of Atonement, in September or October; those who are ill are exempt from fasting.

During Pesarch, the Passover, in March or April, foods that contain yeast including leavened bread, biscuits and cake, are forbidden.

ASSESSING WEIGHT AS A HEALTH RISK

Body mass index

Being overweight or underweight can both have a detrimental effect on health. However, weight as an absolute figure tells us little about the associated risk for the individual patient. The body mass index (BMI) defines weight in terms of health risk by relating weight to height. The BMI is calculated by using the following formula:

$$BMI = \frac{Weight\ (kg)}{Height\ (m)^2}$$

For example, a patient who is 1.64 m tall and who weighs 74 kg has a BMI of:

$$\frac{74}{1.64 \times 1.64} = 27.51$$

To make sense of this figure, the BMI indicates a series of health-related ranges of weight. These are:

- Less than 20.0 = Underweight
- 20.0–24.9 = Acceptable weight
- 25.0–29.9 = Overweight
- 30.0–40.0 = Obese
- More than 40.0 = Severely obese

The patient in the example is, therefore, overweight, which poses some health risks. Graph charts are available that calculate the BMI from direct measurements of height and weight. These can be a useful tool to show patients where their BMI is in relation to the ranges.

It is important to remember that the BMI only relates to a patient's calorie intake and energy expenditure; it does not consider the quality of the diet and how its calories are achieved. For example, alcohol is high in calories but offers little nutritional value.

Waist – hip ratio

The waist – hip ratio is another indicator that can be useful in assessing risk. A high waist–hip ratio (apple shape) is strongly associated with cardiovascular disease, whereas a low waist – hip ratio (pear shape) is strongly associated with non-insulin-dependent diabetes.

To measure the ratio, measure:

- around the body at the widest point of the hips;
- around the waist; if this is ill-defined, use the mid-point between the base of the ribs and the top of the pelvis.

$$\text{Waist–hip ratio} = \frac{\text{waist measurement}}{\text{hip measurement}}$$

A waist–hip ratio of more than 1.0 in men or 0.8 in women is an indicator of increased risk of cardiovascular disease. This applies even if the person is only slightly overweight.

WEIGHT REDUCTION

Patients with a BMI over 25.0 should be encouraged to reduce weight steadily at a rate of 0.5–1 kg (1–2 lb) per week. Those with special needs – the obese, the severely obese, children and expectant and nursing mothers – should be referred to a dietitian.

STRATEGIES FOR A HEALTHIER DIET

Any psychological cause of weight problems should be identified and addressed, whether weight is a real or perceived concern. The BMI can be a useful objective tool to help distinguish psychological and physiological evidence.

For most people, there are several main dietary principles to follow to eat a healthier diet. It is important that these are discussed and advised only once any medical conditions have been explored, as the latter may totally refute some of these guidelines:

- Enjoy the food being eaten.
- Eat a variety of different foods to gain a balance of nutrients.
- Increase the level of fibre, by eating, for example wholemeal bread, fruit and vegetables, pulses, wholegrain cereal, brown rice and wholemeal pasta.
- Decrease fat intake, for example by using a low fat spread, using skimmed milk, grilling rather than frying food and avoiding fatty meats and snacks.
- Decrease sugar intake, for example by using artificial sweeteners rather than sugar, avoiding sweets, chocolate and biscuits and using diet versions of soft drinks.
- Decrease the consumption of alcohol. This is high in calories and low in nutrients. Its effects also help to weaken resolve.
- Decrease salt intake by not using salt in cooking, not adding salt at the table, reducing the intake of processed and convenience foods or opting for low-salt alternatives.

Patients are more likely to be over- than underweight. If overweight, they should reduce their calorie intake and increase exercise, as appropriate to their medical condition. It is important to consider all calories consumed: alcohol and some soft drinks can be high in calories and should be either limited or replaced by low calorie alternatives.

Losing a significant amount of weight can take many months, so it is important to set achievable short-term targets to avoid loss of morale and increase confidence in the ability to lose weight. Although short-term 'crash' diets may seem attractive, they do not re-educate people towards a new pattern of eating, so it is likely that they will return to their old eating habits and, therefore, increase their weight following the diet:

- Long-term change is more important than short-term 'crash' diets.
- The diet is more likely to succeed in the long term if normal foods are eaten rather than special diet bars and meal replacements, as these do not re-educate towards a permanent healthier diet.
- A food diary can be useful in helping the patient to realise how much food is being consumed and when during the day. Often, people may be surprised at the actual amount that is eaten when it is written down.
- Aim for a realistic safe weight loss; from this, goals for significant dates can be set, for example losing 4 kg for a family wedding.
- A slimming club is helpful for some people; there they can meet others for mutual support and be encouraged to stick to a diet.
- Shopping for food after having just eaten a main meal rather than when hungry can reduce the temptation to buy such food as biscuits, cakes and confectionery.

- Shopping should be from a list derived from a planned menu to avoid temptation.
- Increasing exercise increases the amount of energy and thus calories expended. Overweight people benefit greatly from exercise as they burn up more calories than a thinner person because of moving a heavier body.
- Rewards can act as something to look forward to after specific weight losses. These should not be food but need not be expensive; for example a reward could be a magazine that is not usually bought or a trip out somewhere special.
- The diet should not be abandoned if it is broken. The occasional slip is probably not harmful to the overall pattern of eating. It need not be the end of the diet − start again the next day.

FOOD LABELLING

Food labels must, by law, provide detailed information about what the food is and its constituent ingredients.

Nutritional information is provided by many manufacturers, although it is not required by law. However, it can be useful for example, comparing labels on two tins of baked beans from different manufacturers enables the healthier brand to be chosen. So that comparisons can be made, labels show how much of a nutrient there is in 100 g of the product. It is important to remember to relate this to the weight of the tin or packet to find the total number of calories or amount of a nutrient that would be consumed. For example, a particular tin of baked beans weighs 425 g. It contains 64 kilocalories per 100 g. The total calorie content of the tin is thus:

$$\frac{425 \times 64}{100} = 272 \text{ kilocalories}$$

If only half the tin were eaten, the person would consume $272 \div 2 = 136$ kilocalories.

Energy can also be given in kilojoules (kJ), a more modern measure of energy than kilocalories.

'Use by', 'Best before' and 'Sell by' dates

These dates appear on many food products. The 'Use by' date is a definite date that is displayed on the packaging of perishable foods and is the date by which the food should be eaten. If not eaten by this date, the food should be thrown away. However, this date is not a guarantee that the food has not already perished, as decay also depends on the temperature the food is stored at.

The 'Best before' date is a guide to when the food will be at its best in terms of taste, texture and safety.

The 'Sell by' date is a date beyond which it is illegal to sell that particular item. Again, it is not a guarantee that the food has not perished prior to that date. This term is becoming less common in an attempt to clarify the confusion that has arisen from the variety of dates that are displayed on food and their different implications.

Food safety

The safety of the food that is eaten should be considered:

- Observe 'Use by' dates.
- Store food at the correct temperature, as advised on the packaging, to delay decay, and check the temperature of refrigerators and freezers.
- Check that the packaging is intact.
- Observe basic rules of hygiene, for example hand washing.
- Cook food thoroughly to destroy any harmful organisms that may be present in the food.
- Do not reheat food more than once, as this encourages the growth of harmful organisms.

BARRIERS TO HEALTHY EATING

Gimmick diets

Satiety, the state of inhibition over further eating, is in part specific to a particular food that has been consumed, so the availability of a variety of palatable foods will prolong eating and increase energy intake and may ultimately lead to obesity. Many gimmick diets rely on this fact by radically restricting the foods that are 'allowed', so that the person becomes bored with the food and eats less.

Although these types of diet might have a result in the short term, weight is usually regained as long-term eating patterns have not been changed. If these diets are followed for too long, health-threatening depletions in nutrients can occur, as the range of food eaten is too narrow.

Very low-calorie diets

These lead to a rapid weight loss. The body adjusts to this by lowering the metabolic rate, so that any food eaten is used to greater potential, which is a response to starvation. Thus, once 'normal eating' is resumed, weight gain is rapid.

Cost

Healthy eating is often thought of as expensive. However, this need not be the case, and it can work out cheaper than buying prepared foods and snacks:

- Fruit and vegetables are cheap when bought in season.
- Branded 'healthy foods' can be more expensive than unmarked equivalents, which may be nutritionally as good.
- 'Ordinary' fruit and vegetables are just as nutritious as 'exotic' ones and are considerably cheaper.
- Frozen foods may work out cheaper than the fresh equivalent.
- It costs nothing financially to cut excess fat off meat, but it may be cheaper to buy lean meat as then there is no waste.
- Switching to wholemeal versions of foods such as bread and pasta may not be more expensive.

Attitude

The easiest way of failing to eat a healthy diet is to try to eat foods that are disliked. It is important to find a diet that fits in with lifestyle and taste preferences. There is no point trying to persuade patients to eat a disliked food or give up a food that is particularly liked, as they will not keep to the diet. It is the overall diet over a period of time that is most significant for being healthy.

Taste can be modified over time, for example by slowly reducing the amount of sugar in cups of tea. Even a small change can result in great benefit when multiplied by the number of cups of tea consumed each day. Many people could manage to reduce the amount of sugar in their tea but could not cope with the idea of not taking any sugar.

Time

Not all convenience foods are nutritionally unsound. There are a variety of convenience foods that are very healthy, for example:

- baked beans;
- all fruit and vegetables, particularly those eaten raw;
- semi-skimmed and skimmed milk;
- dried fruit;
- tinned sardines and tuna (not preserved in oil);
- low-fat yoghurts.

Knowledge

Experts are sometimes uncertain of and do not always agree on particular aspects of nutrition and their relationship to disease. These issues are sometimes exaggerated in the media. However, although there are some areas of uncertainty and disagreement, for example the debate surrounding cholesterol and its relevance to heart disease, there are many areas over which experts do agree. It is important to focus on these with patients rather than using the other areas as an excuse to avoid dietary issues.

SPECIFIC DISORDERS WITH NUTRITIONAL IMPLICATIONS

Dietitians are the expert health-care professionals in hospital for patients with dietary problems. The policy in one's place of work as to when patients should be referred to the dietitian should be studied. However, if the nurse is in any doubt, she should not attempt to advise patients beyond her knowledge or understanding. It is important to determine the type of support and advice offered to patients from the dietitian in a particular hospital, as practice varies between settings. This means that the best support can be offered to the patient by working in partnership with the dietitian, so that:

- advice given to a patient is consistent between professionals;
- the patient feels secure that the professionals agree, as research shows that this is a common cause of concern;
- there are no 'gaps' where both the nurse and the dietitian think that something has been discussed with the patient by the other.

Coronary heart disease and stroke

Obesity is a predisposing factor for coronary heart disease and stroke, so patients who are overweight should be encouraged to lose weight.

Salt intake is an important factor in setting blood pressure, and lowering salt intake has been shown to reduce hypertension. Consumption often vastly exceeds actual body requirements, with the average person eating about 10 g per day, when the recommended intake is 6 g per day.

Diabetes mellitus

Diabetes mellitus is a common condition, affecting over one million people in the UK. It is the result of either reduced production or a complete lack of insulin, so the body is unable to utilise sugar.

Although diabetes cannot be cured, it can be well controlled by diet alone or diet combined with oral hypoglycaemic drugs or insulin. Patients who are newly diagnosed diabetics and their families often find dietary advice difficult to absorb, as they have to learn new ways of looking at food, considering not only the amount and type of food but also how it is cooked and when it is eaten. The dietitian will probably be involved with the family's care, so it is important that advice and support are given in conjunction with the dietitian to ensure that messages are consistent and not contradictory.

Dietary advice needs to relate to the particular needs of each patient. However, the overall aim is to balance the levels of sugar and insulin in the bloodstream in order to avoid the complications that arise from the excess of one over the other. General guidelines are very similar to those for anyone eating a healthy diet:

- Avoid being overweight.
- Eat regular meals.
- Limit salt intake.
- Eat high fibre carbohydrates.
- Avoid too much fat, choosing polyunsaturated and mono-unsaturated fats in preference to saturated fats.
- Eat about 400 g of fruit and vegetables each day.

Special diabetic foods are not recommended as they are expensive and unnecessary; instead low sugar alternatives, for example of squashes, desserts and tinned fruit, can be suggested.

Coeliac disease

Coeliac disease is a malabsorption syndrome. Gliadin, one of the proteins in gluten, interferes with the uptake of nutrients by the mucosa of the small intestine. The mucosal cells become flat instead of columnar and lose their villi. This results in a small smaller surface area for the absorption of nutrients.

Living with coeliac disease involves avoiding wheat and gluten in the diet. Many manufacturers now label gluten-free foods on the packaging, making them easier to recognise:

The Coeliac Society (see Appendix 2) may be a useful source of information and support.

HOSPITAL POLICIES AND NUTRITION

Information about healthy eating abounds, but, in order to make changes towards a healthier diet, healthy food must obviously be available. By making healthy food easily available and attractively presented, healthy eating becomes an easier option and one that people are more likely to choose.

A healthy eating policy for hospital staff could result in:

- healthier and more energetic staff;
- less diet-related illness;
- staff feeling more valued;
- an increase in income from the staff dining room as more staff choose to eat there;
- a greater awareness of the relationships between diet and health.

Asking patients and staff about the type of food they would like available can be a good starting point. This helps people to feel involved as it becomes 'their policy' rather than a change that is forced upon them.

Improvements to the diets of patients and staff could encompass the following:

- Healthy food choices could be marked on menus, indicating, for example, low fat, high fibre and low salt choices. A simpler method for the staff menu would be to mark a 'healthy meal', but this would be inappropriate for patients as it might not be a 'healthy meal' for them.
- Several sizes of serving could be made available. Elderly patients who are sedentary require a very different diet from a physically active patient in hospital for a short stay. Clerical staff who spend long periods of time sitting at a desk need fewer calories than a porter constantly walking and lifting.

More in-patients complain about the food available than about any other aspect of their care, so a healthy eating policy should make patients feel happier about their hospital stay, as well as contributing towards their physical recovery.

6

Physical Activity

Modern sedentary lifestyles tend to lead to a lack of fitness and physical activity unless positive actions are taken to take exercise. Approximately 80% of men and 90% of women are in occupations that do not require at least moderately vigorous physical activity.

Fitness is a combination of factors. The main components are muscle strength, joint flexibility, endurance ability, stamina, skill and a healthy diet. Fitness capability declines quickly if activity levels fall, for example following a period of bedrest.

INCIDENCE AND TRENDS IN PHYSICAL ACTIVITY

The Allied Dunbar Fitness Survey (1992, see Appendix 3) found that 70% of men and 80% of women were less active for their age than they should be in order to achieve a health benefit. In contrast, 80% of people believed themselves to be fit, the majority incorrectly considering that they exercised sufficiently. The implications for health care professionals are:

- educating people on the levels of appropriate exercise for them;
- helping them to fulfil these targets.

HEALTH GAINS OF PHYSICAL ACTIVITY

General health

The risk to general health and well-being from inactivity is serious. There is a progressive loss of capacity for physical work through decreased aerobic fitness and muscle weakness. Joints become stiff from insufficient movement, so simple movements such as reaching across to put on a car seat belt become a strain.

The elderly

Physical inactivity in the elderly can often lead to physical disability and can make existing conditions worse. However, this type of disability need not be inevitable and is often reversible, through appropriate exercise programmes based on individual pre-existing capabilities and limitations.

Stamina

Stamina depends on the ability of the heart and lungs to deliver oxygen and on the efficiency with which muscles can use it. Any continuous activity that requires faster deeper respirations helps to improve stamina. This type of physical activity is termed aerobic exercise, as it relies on effective and efficient use of oxygen. Activities particularly good at increasing stamina are cycling, running, swimming and brisk walking.

Muscular strength

Physical activity that improves strength helps to protect the body from sprains and strains. Movements should be repeated several times, slightly raising the pulse rate. Activities particularly good at increasing muscular strength are cycling, running, swimming and weight training.

Flexibility, suppleness and stretching

Suppleness is the ability to bend, stretch, twist and turn body parts through the full range of natural movement. This can be achieved through either specific physical activities or daily activities. To be effective, this exercise should be done smoothly and slowly, with the pulse rate remaining steady. Activities particularly good at increasing flexibility and suppleness are swimming and yoga.

Coordination

Movement can help to improve coordination, and practice increases dexterity and ability. Activities particularly suitable for increasing general coordination are swimming, dancing, badminton and tennis.

DISEASES AND PHYSICAL ACTIVITY

Cardiovascular disease

An association has been shown between high levels of physical activity and a low incidence of coronary heart disease. Regular exercise improves the condition of the heart muscles. Stronger contractions mean that the heart is working more efficiently, so it does not have to beat so often, thus reducing the strain on the heart. This reduces the risks of myocardial infarction and stroke.

Hypertension can be controlled, to some extent, by exercise. Adults with mild or labile arterial hypertension have been shown to have reductions in both systolic and diastolic blood pressure of, on average, 12 mmHg through taking regular moderate rhythmic exercise.

Dietary disorders

Regular physical activity can help both to prevent obesity, which exacerbates the effects of many diseases, and to reduce obesity in overweight people. With obesity, there is a greater risk of developing hypertension, heart disease and late-onset diabetes. Obese people are twice as likely to die before the age of 65 than is a person of normal weight. The very obese will experience a reduced exercise tolerance, so have to exercise gently.

Glucose tolerance deteriorates with increasing age and is exacerbated by obesity, but exercise can help to reverse this. The prevalence of impaired glucose tolerance is less among active people.

Metabolic control

Moderate exercise appears to reduce the risk of developing diabetes for both normal weight and obese middle-aged people. For those who have already developed maturity-onset diabetes, exercise can ameliorate the disease by increasing insulin sensitivity. Sufficient regular vigorous exercise, combined with dietary control, may prevent the need for insulin injections.

Bone density

Low activity levels during childhood increase the risk of fractures in later years, as childhood and adolescence is the time that skeletal bone mass increases, making bones stronger.

Bone mass decreases after the fourth decade. In post-menopausal women, the rate of loss accelerates for several years. Osteoporosis due to low bone density can particularly result in fractures of the vertebra or femur. Women aged 50–75 years who have a low bone density are 60 times more likely to suffer a fractured neck of femur than similar aged women with normal bone density. Weight bearing exercise can increase bone density, even after the menopause.

Rheumatoid arthritis

Exercises that emphasise stretching and muscle strength have been shown to alleviate symptoms of rheumatoid arthritis and reduce the need for medication. However, exercise is contraindicated when the disease is in an acute phase or if pain persists after exercise.

PHYSICAL ACTIVITY AND PREGNANCY

During pregnancy, the general health benefits of physical activity still apply. Moderate exercise during pregnancy is associated with a lower incidence of premature birth. It does not appear adversely to affect birth weight or length of gestation.

Those unaccustomed to exercise should not, during pregnancy, start new activities other than walking and swimming; many sports centres now run specific antenatal aquarobics classes. Some sports are inadvisable, such as riding, where there is risk of falling off a horse. As with all physical activity, the greatest benefit comes from the most appropriate form of exercise, taking into account previous fitness levels, injuries and medical condition.

THE PHYSIOLOGICAL EFFECT OF PHYSICAL ACTIVITY

Regular exercise has been shown to lead to significant changes in biochemical and physiological function. These changes:

- help to prevent disease;
- have a favourable effect on the progression of the disease;
- ameliorate the effects of chronic disease.

The pulse rate can be used as a guide to the intensity of exercise. It is a useful indicator as it is a personal guide, the same activity having very different effects on different people, depending on their level of fitness, but is not particularly helpful for people taking medication that affects the pulse rate, for example beta blockers. After exercise, the pulse rate should return to the normal resting rate within three minutes. If it does not, exertion has been too great and emphasis should be placed on increasing cardiovascular capability, for example, by brisk walking.

Carbohydrate and fat are both utilised during aerobic activity, the proportions depending on the type of activity. Aerobic activity is thus recommended for weight loss, as fat stores are reduced. This use of fat conserves glycogen, so aerobic activity can continue for some while. Eventually, depending on the individual, this aerobic supply of energy becomes inadequate for the activity to continue, and anaerobic metabolism, work without oxygen, is necessary. If sufficient oxygen is unavailable, energy is obtained in the short term by the breakdown of creatinine phosphate in the muscle and the conversion of glycogen, stored in the muscle, to lactate. The lactate leads to fatigue and aching muscles.

During physical activity, blood flow is increased so that more oxygen, glucose and fat are delivered to the muscles, while removing more carbon dioxide and lactate. This is achieved by:

- increased cardiac output – the pulse rate rises;
- dilatation of arteries and arterioles in the muscles;
- increased blood flow from the viscera to the muscles and to the skin to increase heat loss.

THE PSYCHOLOGICAL EFFECTS OF PHYSICAL ACTIVITY

Physical activity of appropriate intensity, frequency and duration confers psychological benefits:

- It helps people to relax and cope with stress more effectively and improves sleep patterns.
- By feeling fitter, self-esteem is raised.
- Improvements in memory have been shown with exercise, particularly for the elderly.
- It has been found to reduce mild depression and anxiety. Evidence is uncertain as to whether this is due to social changes, for example contact with others, to diversion or due to the effects of endorphins on the central nervous system.

THE SOCIAL EFFECT OF PHYSICAL ACTIVITY

Contact with others through team or group activities and classes can help to form new friendships and provides a diversion. Physical activity should be fun and enjoyable!

Some sports and leisure centres offer crèches and child care facilities, so that those with pre-school children can take part, meeting others and helping to ameliorate isolation. There are also often sessions run specifically for those over 50 years old.

Although there are great benefits to be gained from physical activity, specific advice needs to be sought from specialists for people with specific conditions, for example:

- those with a history of cardiac disease;
- those with arthritis or bone or joint disorders, where specific exercises may aggravate the disease;
- grossly obese people, whose exercise tolerance will be low;
- those with respiratory disorders, as oxygen intake may be impaired.

For these people, exercise itself is not precluded, but rather the emphasis is on a gentle programme, advised by specialists, that slowly builds up fitness.

There are several obstacles to increasing physical activity, but these can be overcome through planning:

- Choose an activity that is enjoyable. Exercise should be fun, not an endurance.
- If time is short, plan exercise as part of other activities, for example, running upstairs instead of walking.
- Physical activity should not be seen as an alternative to relaxation, as it actually helps relaxation and improves sleep patterns.
- Exercise should not hurt; if it does, stop. If a 'burning sensation' is experienced, this is the time to stop, before any pain is felt. Most injuries are caused by overuse of joints and muscles, so build up to more vigorous exercise slowly over a few weeks.
- Age and health are not barriers to becoming fitter. It is a matter of finding the appropriate form of exercise.
- Always warm up gently before strenuous physical activity, to lessen the risk of injury. This prepares both the muscles and the mind for exercise.
- After vigorous exercise, do not stop suddenly but cool down by walking around and doing gentle stretching movements, holding the stretches for 15–20 seconds, to allow the body to recover.

SPECIFIC PHYSICAL ACTIVITIES

Walking, jogging and running

Walking is the most natural form of exercise. It increases stamina and strengthens leg muscles. To increase the amount walked:

- take the stairs instead of the lift;
- walk instead of drive for short journeys;
- join a club and walk with others.

Power walking is a particularly good way of increasing cardiovascular fitness. For this, the walker alternates 20 normal speed paces with 20 fast ones.

Walking is not only free, but can save money on petrol and bus fares. No special equipment is necessary, unless hill walking is envisaged. For hill walking:

- wear strong, comfortable shoes and thick warm socks;
- wear several layers of thin clothes rather than one thick layer;
- use a waterproof coat for protection from wind and rain;
- take expert advice when necessary;
- tell someone the planned route and approximate return time.

Playing golf can entail walking four to five miles and can improve stamina and leg strength.

Jogging also improves stamina, although there is a risk of overuse injuries to feet, knees, ankles, the spine and hips. This risk is decreased by:

- not running too far at first;
- running on soft surfaces;
- wearing a good pair of running shoes with a cushioned sole to prevent jarring and good arch support;
- not running on just the toes, but using heels as well;

Other risks are from traffic and lack of personal safety, and can be reduced by:

- wearing light coloured clothes or reflective bands;
- running in well-lit areas;
- running with others.

Swimming

Swimming is the best activity for all round fitness. It increases stength, stamina and suppleness, particularly if a variety of strokes are used. For swimming:

- there is no age barrier to either swimming or learning to swim;
- many swimming pools have special sessions, for example over 50s, adults only and parents and babies;

- there are often special rates for the unwaged and retired;
- warming up before and gentle stretches after swimming reduce the risk of injury.

Cycling

Cycling increases stamina, strengthens muscles and can help weight reduction. Like walking, it is an activity that can be undertaken individually or as part of a group. For cycling:

- wear a bicycle helmet;
- ensure that the saddle is at the correct height. When the foot is at the lowest point on the pedal, the knee should be slightly bent, which allows for a full range of joint movement;
- wear light-coloured or reflective clothes at night, and ensure lights are in good working order;
- follow the *Highway Code*;
- maintain the bicycle, particularly checking the brakes;
- arrange for children to take cycling proficiency tests (contact the public safety or road safety department of the local council);
- follow special cycle paths and routes away from the main traffic routes, if these are available.

Dance and movement to music

Dancing increases strength, particularly of leg muscles, and improves stamina, joint suppleness and mobility, coordination and balance. For dancing:

- special shoes or clothes may be necessary; the teacher can give specific advice on what is required;
- not all forms require a partner: some are group dances, for example, folk, while others are individual, for example, ballet;
- classes are often available through adult education institutes and leisure centres;
- there are often special rates for the unwaged and retired;
- it can be a good way of making new friends.

Gym-based physical activity

Many different forms of physical activity are gym based, including circuit training, exercise classes and weight training.

Most gyms insist on a fitness test and induction before any equipment is used; this ensures that the right form of activity is chosen and programmes can be personalised to take existing fitness and medical conditions into consideration. If a fitness test and induction programme are not offered, find another gym where the emphasis is placed on safety.

Aerobics and keep fit classes are usually offered at various levels. They combine jogging and jumping movements with strengthening and stretching exercises to give a general work-out.

'Look after Yourself' classes are widely available in England, Wales and some areas of Scotland. These offer a combination of exercise to music and advice on relaxation, coping with stress and healthy eating.

Weight training can be with either free weights or machines, and can increase strength and suppleness. It is vital that correct lifting techniques are taught and practised to prevent injury.

Yoga

Yoga teaches control over movements and breathing. Through gentle controlled movements, it improves suppleness and flexibility and assists relaxation. There is no age barrier to yoga.

Physical activity in the home

There are a variety of ways to improve physical fitness at home, although the social benefit of meeting others and sharing experiences is lost.

- A wide range of exercise tapes and books is available from bookshops. Some libraries also stock these. Tapes are generally easier to follow than trying to read a book and perform an exercise at the same time.
- Running up and down stairs, on the spot or in the garden can be incorporated into everyday activities around the house.
- Bicycle and rowing machines improve stamina, but can be expensive. It is important to try them out before buying, as there are several different designs on the market.

Physical activity in the home is probably unsupervised, so it is important to be aware of some safety precautions:

- Beginners would benefit from an instructor to correct body alignment and advise on the most appropriate level and type of exercise.
- It is inadvisable to take vigorous exercise if infection or pyrexia is present.
- At least two hours should be left following a meal before undertaking vigorous exercise.

- All activities should start with a gentle warm-up, and exercises should be built up slowly to prevent injury.
- Any uncertainties on the appropriateness or degree of an exercise should be referred to a qualified professional.
- If an activity hurts or if breathlessness prevents carrying on a conversation, stop, remembering to slow down gradually.

BARRIERS TO BEING HEALTHIER

Exercise can be unsafe if:

- it is too strenuous;
- it is performed erratically. Sedentary people have 30 times the risk of having a primary cardiac arrest during unaccustomed vigorous exertion than do people who are frequently active;
- warning signs and symptoms are ignored. Many sports are competitive by nature, so participants may be disinclined to stop playing and consequently ignore warning symptoms. In 45 of the 51 deaths from coronary heart disease between 1976 and 1984 associated with playing squash, the player had ignored chest pain.

HOSPITAL POLICIES AND PHYSICAL ACTIVITY

Physical activity can make a major contribution to the physical and psychological well-being of hospital staff by improving muscular strength, flexibility and stamina and by relieving stress.

The most commonly cited obstacles by hospital staff against taking up physical activity in the hospital are:

- lack of facilities;
- pressure of work. This is when relaxation or yoga classes would be of great benefit;
- cost.

However, a progressive policy on physical activity could help to overcome these barriers and constructively improve the health of staff. Such a policy could:

- help staff to be more relaxed and productive;
- improve working relationships between staff;
- maintain and improve staff fitness levels;
- reduce the number of working days lost to sickness related to physical inactivity and lack of fitness;
- reduce the incidence of back injuries.

Some hospitals allow staff to use patient facilities when not in use, for example, a swimming pool primarily for physiotherapy that would otherwise be unused in the early mornings, evenings and weekends. Shift work whereby staff can swim before or after a span of duty, is ideally suited to this arrangement.

A staff survey is often a good place to start when trying to address physical activity issues. It might cover, for example:

- What facilities would staff use?
- At what times?
- What types of activity would staff like to be offered?
- Are there adequate shower facilities?
- Are there existing facilities that could be used more productively?
- Is there secure bicycle parking so that staff are encouraged to cycle rather than drive?

As well as the hospital as a potential site, there are also the possibilities offered by sports facilities, gyms and health clubs. They may be open to corporate membership, allowing for a cheaper and wider use of facilities.

Appendix 1

Health Promotion: Courses, Qualifications and Further Reading

This appendix does not claim to be a fully comprehensive list, as new courses are always being developed and existing courses changed. Most of these courses are multidisciplinary.

COURSES

Postgraduate diplomas

Bath College of Higher Education,
   Newton Park, Bath BA2 9BN
   Tel: (01225) 873701
   (validated by the University of Bath)

Department of Health Science,
   University of Central England, Perry Bar, Birmingham B42 2SU
   Tel: 0121–331 5000

University of the West of England,
   Coldharbour Lane, Frenchay, Bristol BS16 1QY
   Tel: (0117) 965 6261 ext 2351

Christ Church College,
   North Homes Road, Canterbury, Kent CT1 1QU
   Tel: (01227) 767700

Health Education Unit,
   School of Health, Leeds Metropolitan University, Calverley Street,
   Leeds LS1 3HE
   Tel: (0113) 283 2600 ext 3435

Centre for Education Studies,
   Kings College, University of London, 552 Kings Road, London SW10
   0UA
   Tel: 0171–836 5454

Faculty of Medicine,
   University of Manchester, Stopford Building, Oxford Road,
   Manchester M13 9PT
   Tel: 0161–275 5210

School of Education and Nursing Studies,
   University of the Southbank, 103 Borough Road, London SE1 0AA
   Tel: 0171–928 8989

Masters degrees in health promotion/education

These courses are usually one year full time or two years part time.

Bath College of Higher Education,
   Newton Park, Bath BA2 9BN
   Tel: (01225) 873701
   (validated by the University of Bath)

Department of Health Sciences,
   University of Central England, Perry Bar, Birmingham B42 2SU
   Tel: 0121–331 5000

Faculty of Health,
   University of East Sussex, Falmer, Brighton BN1 9HP
   Tel: (01273) 643476

University of the West of England, Coldharbour Lane, Frenchay, Bristol
   BS16 1QY
   Tel: (0117) 965 6261 ext 2351

Department of Community Medicine,
   Edinburgh University, Teviot Place, Edinburgh EH10 9AG
   Tel: 0131–650 1000

Health Education Unit,
   School of Health, Leeds Metropolitan University, Calverley Street,
   Leeds LS1 3HE
   Tel: (0113) 283 2600 ext 3435

School of Education,
  Southampton University, Southampton SO9 5NH
  Tel: (01703) 595000

West London Institute of Higher Education,
  Brunel University, Gordon House, 300 St Margaret's Road,
  Twickenham, Middlesex TW1 1PT
  Tel: 0181–891 0121

Centre for Education Studies,
  Kings College, University of London, 552 Kings Road, London SW10
  0UA
  Tel: 0171–836 5454

London School of Hygiene and Tropical Medicine,
  University of London, Keppel Street, London WC1E 7HT
  Tel: 0171–927 2239

Faculty of Medicine,
  University of Manchester, Stopford Building, Oxford Road,
  Manchester M13 9PT
  Tel: 0161–275 5210

University of Wales College of Medicine, Brunel House, 2 Fitzalan Road,
  Cardiff CF2 1EB
  Tel: (01222) 72472

Department of Health Studies,
  University of East London, Romford Road, London E15 4LZ
  Tel: 0181–590 7722

MA in curriculum studies with an option in health education

Advanced Studies Department,
  University of London, Institute of Education, 20 Bedford Way, London
  WC1H 0AL
  Tel: 0171–636 1500

Masters degrees in public health

Department of Public Health,
  Aberdeen University, Medical School, Foresterhill, Aberdeen AB9 22D
  Tel: (01224) 681818 ext 53727

Postgraduate Office,
  Dundee University, Dundee DD1 4HN
  Tel: (01382) 23181

Department of Community Medicine,
  Glasgow University, 2 Lilybank Gardens, Glasgow G12 8RZ
  Tel: 0141–330 4037

Department of Community Medicine,
  Liverpool University, PO Box 147, Liverpool L69 3BX
  Tel: 0151–794 5575

Board of Public Health Studies,
  University of Wales College of Medicine, Heath Park, Cardiff CF4
  4XN
  Tel: (01222) 755944

Short courses in health promotion/disease prevention

Royal Institute of Public Health and Hygiene,
  28 Portland Place, London W1N 4DE
  Tel: 0171–580 2731

Institute of Advanced Nursing Education,
  Royal College of Nursing, 20 Cavendish Square, London W1M 0AB
  Tel: 0171–409 3333

Specialised courses

Helping people to stop smoking tutor training course:

Stop Smoking,
  PO Box 100, Plymouth PL1 1RG
  Tel: (01752) 709506

Smoke Stop tutor training course:
  Smoke Stop, Department of Psychology, Southampton University,
  Southampton SO9 5NH
  Tel: (01703) 583741

Appendix 2

Sources of Health Promotion Information

GENERAL

Each country in the UK has a national body specialising in health promotion resources and publishing booklets, factsheets, resource packs, videos and posters on health promotion issues.

Health Education Authority,
   Hamilton House, Mabledon Place, London WC1H 9TX
   Tel: 0171–383 3833

Health Promotion Agency for Northern Ireland,
   18 Ormeau Avenue, Belfast BT2 8HS
   Tel: (01232) 311611

Health Education Board for Scotland,
   Woodburn House, Canaan Lane, Edinburgh EH10 4SG
   Tel: 0131–447 8044

Health Promotion Wales,
   Ffynnon-las, Ty Glas Avenue, Llanishen, Cardiff CF4 5DZ
   Tel: (01222) 752222

CORONARY HEART DISEASE AND STROKE

The Family Heart Association is a registered charity that produces fact sheets relating to different aspects of heart disease. It aims to increase awareness of familial hypercholesterolaemia and hyperlipidaemia.

Family Heart Association,
Wesley House, 7 High Street, Kidlington, Oxford OX5 2DH
Tel: (01865) 70292

The Flora Project for Heart Disease Prevention produces a range of leaflets on different lifestyle issues related to coronary heart disease.

The Flora Project for Heart Disease Prevention,
24–28 Bloomsbury Way, London WC1A 2PX
Tel: 0171–831 6262

The British Heart Foundation encourages and finances research into the causes, prevention and treatment of heart disease. It publishes booklets for patients.

British Heart Foundation,
14 Fitzhardinge Street, London W1H 4DH
Tel: 0171–935 0185

Look After Your Heart,
Look After Yourself Project Centre,
Christ Church College, Canterbury, Kent CT1 1QU
Tel: (01227) 455564

The Coronary Prevention Group offers information and advice on the prevention of myocardial infarction.

Coronary Prevention Group,
60 Great Ormond Street, London WC1 3HR
Tel: 0171–833 3687

National Form for Coronary Heart Disease Prevention,
Hamilton House, Mabledon Place, London WC1 9TX
Tel: 0171–383 7638

Chest, Heart and Stroke Association,
CHSA House, 65 North Castle Street, Edinburgh EH2 3LT
Tel: 0131–225 6963

The Stroke Assocation offers practical help to people following a stroke.

The Stroke Association,
CHSA House, 123/7 Whitecross Street, London EC1 8JJ
Tel: 0171–490 7999

CANCER

BACUP (British Association of Cancer United Patients) is an information service staffed by experienced oncology nurses; it also produces booklets.

BACUP,
   3 Bath Place, Rivington Street, London EC2A 3JR
   Tel: 0171–696 9003
   Info: (0800) 181199

Cancerlink offers emotional support and information on all aspects of cancer.

Cancerlink,
   17 Britannia Street, London NW1 4JL
   Tel: 0171–833 2451

WNCCC (Women's Nationwide Cancer Control Campaign) encourages the prevention and early detection of cancer. It produces a wide range of leaflets and an information pack.

WNCCC,
   Suna House, 128–130 Curtain Road, London EC2A 3AR
   Tel: 0171–729 4688

SMOKING

ASH (Action on Smoking and Health) produces publications, including the *ASH Information Bulletin*, a fortnightly current awareness digest of smoking and health related issues. ASH also provides information on running smoking cessation groups, leaflets, books and videos. Send a stamped, self-addressed envelope for a list.

ASH,
   109 Gloucester Place, London W1H 3PH
   Tel: 0171–935 3519

Ciba Geigy produce a Nicotinell TTS support pack, which includes a booklet, an emergency card and a calendar. It is free with the first pack of Nicotinell TTS 30.

Ciba Geigy,
   Wimblehurst Road, Horsham, West Sussex RH12 4AB
   Tel: (01403) 272827

Marion Merrill Dow run a 'Quit smoking programme', which operates via a free registration telephone line for patients who then receive a three-part postal programme of support.

Marion Merrill Dow,
  Lakeside House, Stockley, Uxbridge, Middlesex UB11 1BE
  Tel: (0800) 266622

QUIT is a charity offering help in giving up smoking. It runs 'Quitline', a telephone counselling and information service for ex-smokers and health-care professionals. QUIT produces information packs and can supply carbon monoxide monitors.

QUIT,
  142 Whitchurch Road, London W1H 3DA
  Tel: 0171–487 2858
  Quitline: 0171–487 3000

Smokeline is a free telephone counselling and advice service for people in Scotland who are trying to give up smoking or would like to try. Smokeline can provide a leaflet, 'You can stop smoking', to members of the general public.

Smokeline,
  Tel: (0800) 848484

ALCOHOL

Alcoholics Anonymous (AA) is a self-help group for people with an alcohol problem and a sincere desire to stop drinking. Most meetings are 'closed' to members only, but some are open to professionals who come into contact with people with an alcohol problem through their work. There is a strong committment to anonymity: members' identities are never disclosed and no records of attendance or statistics are kept. No fees are charged.

Alcoholics Anonymous,
  General Service Office, PO Box 1, Stonebow House, Stonebow, York YO1 2NJ
  Tel: (01904) 644026

Alcoholics Anonymous,
  Scottish Office, Baltic Chamber, 50 Wellington Street, Glasgow G2 8HJ
  Tel: 0141–226 2214

Local branch numbers can be found in the telephone directory.

Al-Anon offers support to relatives and friends of people with an alcohol problem, whether that person is still drinking alcohol or not.

Al-Ateen is a confidential self-help support group for young people and teenagers who are affected by someone in the family with an alcohol problem.

Al-Anon and Al-Ateen,
   61 Great Dover Street, London SE1 4YF
   Tel: 0171–403 0888
   Helpline: 0161–343 2737 (24 hour)

Alcohol Concern is a national charity with three main aims:

- To raise public awareness of the problems that alcohol can cause.
- To improve services for people with an alcohol problem.
- To promote preventative action at local and national levels.

Anyone who supports these aims can become a member. Alcohol Concern produces leaflets, information and a bi-monthly journal and maintains a comprehensive library.

Alcohol Concern,
   25 Gray's Inn Road, London WC1X 8FQ
   Tel: 0171–833 3471

Alcohol Concern,
   Ground floor, 4 Dock Chambers, Bute Street, Cardiff CF1 6AG
   Tel: (01222) 488000

Health Search maintains a database of national voluntary and self-help groups.
   Tel: 0131–452 8666

The Medical Council On Alcoholism has an educational and advisory role for health-care professionals. It offers a service to doctors and dentists who have an alcohol problem and can put them in contact with appropriate groups for support and help. It produces leaflets, news-letters and a quarterly journal.

Medical Council on Alcoholism,
   1 St Andrew's Place, London NW1 4LB
   Tel: 0171–487 4445

NUTRITION

British Dietetic Association,
   103 Daimler House, Paradise Street, Birmingham B1 2BJ
   Tel: 0121–643 5483

The Ministry of Agriculture, Fisheries and Food produces a range of leaflets on aspects of food safety.

Food Sense,
  Ministry of Agriculture, Fisheries and Food, London SE99 7TT
  Tel: 0181–694 8862

The Open University runs a course on 'Healthy Eating', which can be followed at home.

Learning Materials Service,
  The Open University, PO Box 188, Milton Keynes MK7 6DH
  Tel: (01908) 655182

The National Dairy Councils produce a range of leaflets and videos about milk and dairy products in relation to health education. They also publish *Nutritional Services Quarterly Review.*

National Dairy Council,
  5–7 John Princes Street, London W1M 0AP
  Tel: 0171–499 7822

Dairy Council for Northern Ireland,
  456 Antrim Road, Belfast BT15 5GB
  Tel: (01232) 770113

Scottish Dairy Council,
  Station House, 34 St Enoch Square, Glasgow G1 4DL
  Tel: 0141–248 6544

The British Diabetic Association produces leaflets and information on diabetes.

The British Diabetic Association,
  10 Queen Anne Street, London W1M 0BD
  Tel: 0171–323 1531

Coeliac Society,
  PO Box 181, London NW2 2QY

British Hyperlipidaemia Association,
  c/o Department of Clinical Biochemistry, The Medical School, Framlington Place, Newcastle upon Tyne NE2 4HH

PHYSICAL ACTIVITY

General

Information about local physical activity facilities can be obtained from

  • local libraries;
  • sports and leisure centres;

- the leisure or recreation department of the local council.

The Sports Council aims to:

- increase participation in sport and physical recreation;
- increase the quantity and quality of sports facilities;
- raise standards of performance;
- provide information for and about sport.

It publishes a wide range of material, both on its own and in conjunction with the Health Education Authority.

The Sports Council,
16 Upper Woburn Place, London WC1 0QP
Tel: 0171–388 1277

British Sports Association for the Disabled can provide information on sports and leisure facilities in specific localities.

British Sports Association for the Disabled,
34 Osnaburgh Street, London NW1 3ND
Tel: 0171–383 7277

Friends of the Earth is an environmental pressure group. It promotes policies to protect the environment, with campaigns on cycling, transport, wildlife and the countryside, energy and pollution.

Friends of the Earth,
377 City Road, London EC1 1NA
Tel: 0171–837 0731

Walking

The Ramblers Association is a registered charity that organises walks and supplies information for those interested in walking. There are over 350 local groups within England, Scotland and Wales.

The Ramblers Association,
1–5 Wandsworth Road, London SW8 2XX
Tel: 0171–582 6878

Swimming

The Amateur Swimming Associations offer information about learning to swim, swimming awards and competitive swimming.

Amateur Swimming Association,
  Harold Fern House, Derby Square, Loughborough LE11 0AL
  Tel: (01509) 230431

Scottish Amateur Swimming Association,
  Holmhills Farm, Greenlees Road, Cambuslang, Glasgow G72 8DT
  Tel: 0141–641 8818

Welsh Amateur Swimming Association,
  Wales Empire Pool, Wood Street, Cardiff CF1 1PP
  Tel: (01222) 344201

The National Co-ordinating Committee on Swimming for the Disabled promotes the use of swimming facilities for the disabled for both recreation and rehabilitation.

National Co-ordinating Committee on Swimming for the Disabled,
  3 Knoll Crescent, Northwood, Middlesex HA6 1HH
  Tel: (01829) 827142

Cycling

Mass cycling extravaganzas and cycling holidays, including the 'Great British Bike Ride' and the 'London to Brighton Bike Ride' are organised by Bike Events.

Bike Events,
  PO Box 75, Bath, Avon

Cycling Touring Club,
  Cotterell House, 69 Meadrow, Godalming, Surrey GU7 3HS
  Tel: (01483) 412217

Riding

Riding for the Disabled provides riding and driving opportunities for disabled people through contact with horses and ponies.

Riding for the Disabled Association,
  Avenue R, National Agricultural Centre, Kenilworth, Warwickshire CV8 2LY
  Tel: (01203) 69510

Appendix 3

Further Reading

HEALTH PROMOTION

Benner P & Wrubel J (1989) *The Primacy of Caring.* California: Addison-Wesley.

Blaxter M (1990) *Health and Lifestyles.* London: Routledge.

Bunton R & Macdonald G (eds) (1992) *Health Promotion: Disciplines and Diversity.* London: Routledge.

Department of Health (1989) *A Strategy for Nursing: A Report of the Steering Committee.* London: Department of Health Nursing Division.

Department of Health (1992) *Health of the Nation: A Strategy for England.* London: HMSO.

Department of Health (1993) *One Year On . . .* London: HMSO.

Department of Health (1993) *Targetting Practice: The Contribution of Nurses, Midwives and Health Visitors.* London: Department of Health.

Dines A & Cribb A (1993) *Health Promotion: Concepts and Practice.* Oxford: Blackwell Scientific.

Downie RS, Fyfe C & Tannahill A (1990) *Health Promotion: Models and Values.* Oxford: Oxford Medical Publications.

Ewles L & Simnett I (1992) *Promoting Health: A Practical Guide.* London: Scutari Press.

McBride A (1994) Health promotion in hospitals: The attitudes, beliefs and practices of hospital nurses. *Journal of Advanced Nursing,* **20**: 92–100.

McBride AS & Moorwood Z (1994) The hospital health promotion facilitator: an evaluation. *Journal of Clinical Nursing* 3: In press.

Macleod Clark J, Wilson-Barnett J, Latter S & Maben J (1992) *Health Education and Health Promotion in Nursing: A Study of Acute Practice Areas.* London: Nursing Studies Department, King's College.

Moon J (1994) A survey of postgraduate courses in health education/promotion. *Health Education Journal,* **53** (1): 100–6.

Rodmell S & Watt A (eds) (1986) *The Politics of Health Education*. London: Routledge.

Royal College of Nursing (1989) *Into the Nineties: Promoting Professional Excellence*. London: Royal College of Nursing.

Tones K, Tilford S & Robinson Y (1991) *Health Education: Effectiveness and Efficiency*. London: Chapman and Hall.

Wilson-Barnett J & Latter S (1993) Factors influencing nurses' health education and health promotion practice in acu:e ward areas. In Wilson-Barnett J & Macleod-Clark J (eds), *Research in Health Promotion and Nursing*. London: Macmillan.

Wilson-Barnett, J & Macleod-Clark J (1993) *Research in Health Promotion and Nursing*. London: Macmillan.

World Health Organisation (1986) *Ottawa Charter for Health Promotion*. Geneva: World Health Organisation.

LIFESTYLE ISSUES

General

The Report of the Director of Public Health is an annual report produced by each Director of Public Health. It can be a useful source of information on the population and services relating to public health and health promotion in each district health authority. It can usually be found in health authority and university libraries.

Smoking

The Royal College of Physicians' report *Smoking and the Young* contains information about the effects of smoking on children and guidance on intervention.

Sanders D (1992) *Smoking Cessation Interventions: Is patient education effective? A review of the literature*. London: London School of Hygiene and Tropical Medicine.

Alcohol

Medical Council on Alcoholism (1989) *Alcohol and Health: a Handbook for Nurses*. London: Medical Council on Alcoholism.

Nutrition

Food Sense, part of the Food Safety Directorate of the Ministry of Agriculture, Fisheries and Food, produces a range of guides on different safety aspects of food.

Food Sense
London   SE99 7TT

Tel: 0181–694 8862

World Health Organisation (1990) *Diet, Nutrition and the Prevention of Chronic Diseases*. Geneva: World Health Organisation.

Committee on the Medical Aspects of Food Policy (COMA) (1984) *Diet and Cardiovascular Disease*. London: DHSS.

This sets out nutritional guidelines and government recommendations for nutritional targets.

A comprehensive list of food legislation material may be obtained from:

Minister of Agriculture, Fisheries and Food
Consumer Protection Division
Nobel House
17 Smith Square
London   SW1P 3JR

Physical Activity

Allied Dunbar (1992) *National Fitness Survey – Summary Report*. London: Health Education Authority.

Index